ONWARDS AND DOWNWARDS

Rachel West

Onwards and Downwards
By Rachel West

A C.B.S. Green Man Publication
Cider Brandy Scribblers
Burnham-on-Sea, Somerset, England

Text copyright @2015 Bren Hall

Ingram Spark 1st edition published in print in the UK
2015 as: Onwards and Downwards
ISBN: 9789082323849

1st digital Kindle edition published on Amazon in
2015 as: Onwards and Downwards
ISBN: 9789082323856

Cover art by Frank Patterson
Cover design by Corin Spinks (Corinography)

All Rights Reserved. No part of this publication may be
reproduced, stored in a retrieval system, or transmitted
in any form or by any means, electronic, mechanical,
photocopying, recording, or otherwise, without the prior
permission of both the copyright owner and the above
publisher of this book.

DEDICATION

With love to
my children
and
grandchildren

PROLOGUE

"A woman must have money and a room of her own if she wants to write fiction" wrote Virginia Woolf in "A Room of One's Own" some years before I was born.

Much as I like her books and admire her as a person, it is Virginia Woolf's Diaries with which I feel most affinity, especially of the years written when she lived in Rodmell, Sussex. This is the village where I was born and raised during my formative years. Unfortunately, too late to have actually met Virginia Woolf, unlike my family who were her neighbours. Some of them worked for both Virginia and her husband Leonard.

This is where my story starts and from then on it is a myriad of memories in no particular order, except they link up in one way or another. Within that, my journey through life progresses from one episode to another making it a potpourri of fact, fiction and bittersweet memories from my cherished childhood and traumatic teenage years - until finally something happened to make me grow up fast, take stock and live with the resulting consequences.

CHAPTER ONE

Virginia sat on the bank with her head in her hands and the stones in her pockets, mesmerised by the fast flowing river. She had left the church after her brothers' memorial service saying she was going for a walk and wanted to be alone. This was it, crunch time. Sink or swim. Her mind was in a whirl and her thoughts were random black invasions. Maybe the tears to release her from the pain of life would come if she sat here for a little while longer. If they didn't, she had already put the stones in her coat pockets and was ready to wade in and sink into oblivion. Virginia heard the church clock strike four and decided to wait until half past to see if the turmoil within her head would stop, or whether she would take the next and final step.

"Please God, make it stop" she cried out loud. Here and now her life was at a crossroads, would it be onwards and upwards or would it be onwards and downwards?

"If you do not tell the truth about yourself, you cannot tell it about other people" wrote Virginia Woolf. My own impression of the truth has never wavered and so I sit and write with no fear or trepidation as the truth will out, come what may.

My great-grandparents, William and Rachel, were born before the turn of last century. He was born and bred in Rodmell, a small farming village on the edge of the South Downs in Sussex, and she was from Lewes, the county town with its medieval castle ruins perched high on a hill. William walked three miles across the fields, past the house Henry VIII gave to Anne Boleyn in Southover, up steep cobbled Keere street to where Rachel lived, where he courted her and then walked home again.

They married in St. Peter's Church in Rodmell and lived in a tied farm cottage at the bottom of the village near the entrance to the Brooks. The Brooks are so called because the River Ouse, which ran the length of Sussex from Slaugham in the north down to the open sea at Newhaven, overflowed at high tide creating water meadows, where cattle and sheep grazed and watercress grew. The Brooks are still there, and are a delightful walk along the river bank, but the river has been given a concrete channel through which to flow so it is drier now, unless it is calling you home or the tides are exceptionally high.

From their home in Briar Cottage my great-grandparents walked up the main road called simply The Street, then along the narrow walled lane past the small school, which was purpose built and consisted of only two rooms, to the church where William was the sexton and Rachel arranged the flowers from their garden. She was one of the few villagers who could read and write so she was also the school mistress until the parish council decided to advertise the position and recruit a spinster from out of town. Parents had to find two pennies a week for their children to go to school then with one penny each for siblings.

On their way to the church they walked past Monks House, which a Mr and Mrs Woolf purchased in 1919 at auction in Lewes for £700, initially as their holiday home from London. Jacob Verrall, the previous owner had wasted away with anorexia nervosa after his wife died, letting his garden overgrow, even though Great-granddad had been his gardener since 1907 and Great-granny took him stews and mashes from her own kitchen.

The new owners were Virginia and Leonard Woolf, the famous authors and members of the Bloomsbury Set, a group of mainly literary friends. They had been renting a house just across the fields in Asheham, as Virginia's sister Vanessa lived in nearby Charleston Farmhouse, but they had been given notice to leave by the owner when they saw Monks House advertised for sale. They did not seem to care that Monks House had no electricity or gas (the village still has no mains gas even now), or that the well for water was in the back garden along with the earth closet outhouse. Bathing would have to be carried out in a tin tub in front of the kitchen range or in the sitting room in front of the fire, whilst washing was managed by a jug and basin in matching china, which have become today's heirlooms or antiques.

Virginia used to write her books and articles, and sporadically enter up her diary in the mornings after breakfast, in her writing lodge at the end of a brick path and under the church wall at the bottom of the garden. She had a fine view of Mount Caburn from there. Leonard also wrote in the mornings but he worked indoors. After lunch Virginia often went for a walk along the river bank or up over the Downs, deep in thought. If she passed any villagers she would not stop and talk, merely replying to their greeting and walking on; she even half-jokingly referred to the villagers as peasants because of her privileged upbringing in a house with servants, her father being Sir Leslie Stephen.

They often had their London friends visit them. In the summer months they played croquet and bowls on the lawn or sat outside Virginia's writing lodge talking. Her sister and her children would sometimes come over to visit from their house across the river. Virginia and Leonard did not have children of their own but they had two dogs, Sally and Pinker, and Leonard had a pet marmoset called Mitz, who travelled with him and ate scraps from their table. Mitz was found dead on Boxing Day 1938 with her tail wrapped around her neck and her eyes shut; Leonard buried her in the snowy garden under a wall.

Great-grandfather became Leonard's gardener and they worked side by side taming the overgrown wilderness. Leonard gardened in the afternoons, weather permitting, and in the evenings after dinner the Woolfs read by lamplight, listened to music or the wireless and Virginia took up her embroidery. As she was brought up with servants, she had no experience of housework and little of cooking. My great-grandmother took them dinners of mashes and stews in deep multi-coloured dishes, swimming in gravy thick with carrots and onions, from her own home in Pear Tree Cottage, when they first moved in because Monks House had no stove or grate. William and Rachel also had an earth closet outhouse and a well, where the water was collected by a bucket on a rope, lowered and raised by turning a handle. That well is still there, but not used of course. They kept chickens and rabbits and grew vegetables, as they had eight children to feed, ten mouths with their own and twelve with the Woolfs. Rachel also grew flowers to decorate the church.

Things progressed for the Woolfs; when Virginia sold a book they were able to have some conveniences installed and they engaged Louie, a village woman as a daily cook cum housekeeper. This was fortuitous because Great-granny Rachel became ill and died. When they were burying her in the churchyard behind Monks House, she was so heavy that the coffin straps snapped and Rachel ended up face down in her grave instead of facing her Lord. The Woolf's housekeeper went to the funeral and told Virginia who noted it in her diary.

Great-granddad William grew too old and infirm to do any more paid gardening so Leonard employed a gardener, Percy, another local villager. After his wife died William moved further up The Street to live with one of his daughters, Dorothy and her husband Fred in Vine Cottages. I remember seeing him in their large side garden behind the flint stone wall, hoeing out weeds, pottering about or sitting outside the shed in the far corner on sunny days, with his walking sticks beside him.

In the 1960's Rodmell had a building boom so nowadays there is a detached house on the old garden plot but Vine Cottages are still there. In previous times it was used as the village post office until that was moved up to the top of The Street across the main road into the old corn store, which is now three large flats in the same odd shaped building next to the old forge.

#######

My granddad Jack didn't actively work for the Woolfs but he was a member of Rodmell Labour Party which Leonard had organised and he used to attend the monthly meetings in Monks House. He and my grandmother Florence had grown apart so he asked Leonard's advice on how to get a divorce. They'd married in 1916 during the First World War and separated just before the Second World War, when their youngest child was fourteen and able to leave school to earn her own keep, mainly by helping her mother run the village shop which was attached to their cottage.

Wars upset and unsettle people, even those who are not directly involved in one.

Virginia with her recurring bouts of depression and migraines, Leonard with his Jewish fear of the Nazi's and my grandparents who struggled and separated. One of their problems was that Gran would not have any more children and being one of nine, who can blame her? She gave us some advice on that subject once – she told me to keep my legs crossed and my husband to tie a knot in it!

Their two sons joined up to serve in World War Two. Ken, my dad, joined the Army, in the Royal Horse Artillery regiment, where he served in Cairo, Egypt until he was invalided home on a hospital ship. He called it a holiday cruise on a postcard home as it was a converted cruise ship. He had several back operations but recovered fully to lead a normal and active life. My uncle Albert and their cousin Roy both joined the Royal Air Force. Roy was an air gunner; one day he got his pilot to fly low over Rodmell by prior arrangement when they were en route, and most of the village turned out to cheer and wave. They also survived the war.

Gran would not give Granddad the divorce he wanted but he went off to live with his mistress Doris anyway – in the same village, no less! However, I don't blame him for seeking love and happiness because he was put into Newhaven Workhouse with his younger brother at the tender age of ten. His father had died and his mother had to move back in with her parents in Lewes road, Newhaven, so there was not enough room or money to keep her two eldest sons with her, as well as her other children.

She married again after a while but my granddad and great-uncle had to live in the Workhouse as scholars, (which meant they were sent to school in Newhaven, the same school that my dad, myself and brothers all attended). As soon as my granddad was able to leave school he joined the Army. He was in the First World War in the 23rd Brigade of the Royal Field Artillery and ended his war as a Corporal in Italy. I never knew that side of the family growing up. I wasn't allowed to, but my dad kept in touch with his father who died in Brighton hospital in the 1950's of a burst stomach ulcer. Gran always swore he died because Doris took him biscuits in hospital which irritated his ulcer and made it bleed.

Gran was a Land Girl during World War Two and known locally as Enemy Flo. In fact, being an older woman, she was in charge of the local land girls. Needs must and doing her bit for the country. My mum was living in Gran's house with me as a baby. I was named Virginia after Mrs Woolf and Rachel after my great-grandmother. Mum had been told by my dad to evacuate from the bombing in London where she had been living with her parents, so my mother kept house and my grandmother went out to work. My unmarried aunt Audrey was still living at home, and was casually employed by the Woolfs to help the Cook when they had their weekend guests and dinner parties. Yes, there was rationing, but everybody managed one way or another. An egg was like gold dust, so people who had the space kept hens, no more than three though or else it was classed as a business. People with no chickens or access to eggs could buy the powdered stuff for cooking as the ration was only one egg a week, or two if you were pregnant or vegetarian.

Aunt Audrey would beg, borrow or buy material to make new clothes with the money she earned, to wear to the village dances. One week she met a Canadian soldier. There were a lot of them billeted around locally and they liked to frequent the Abergavenny Arms, the village pub. They got a donkey so drunk once they had to carry the poor animal home. Her soldier was a sergeant named Jim.

Gran was not happy about this romance, so my aunt left home to go and lodge in the pub. One thing led to another and Aunt Audrey and her soldier had to get married. They tied the knot in Lewes Registry Office.

#######

Virginia Woolf was still suffering from her illnesses in the early 1940's. Having endured WW1 in London, only twenty years later there was another war on. They had moved down to

Rodmell permanently by now because their London homes were bombed out twice. Leonard set up the Hogarth Press in their garage, thinking it would give Virginia something tangible to do alongside her writing. They also kept their car in the garage together with extra petrol cans because Leonard believed that he was on the Nazi hit list. If the Nazis came they were going to kill themselves with car fumes in the garage. Imagine that! That's what war and fear do to people.

One afternoon in March 1941, Virginia wrote Leonard a letter and left it propped up where he would see it when he came indoors. She put on her coat and walked down to the Brooks where she filled her pockets with stones, waded into the river and drowned herself. Leonard read Virginia's note and went out looking for her but to no avail, so he alerted the village policeman PC Collins, who called in the Chief Air Raid Warden Mr Freeth, and other village men, one of whom was Frank Dean the blacksmith, and they all searched for her. But they could not find her anywhere.

On 18th April 1941 some teenaged friends, three boys and two girls, were cycling from Lewes to Seaford when they stopped to eat their sandwiches along the river bank. The boys saw a log floating in the river so they started throwing stones at it until one of the boys realised it wasn't a log. He waded in and overturned it with a stick to see it was a woman in a fur coat. They went off and rang the police then the boys waited but sent the girls home. They did not know it then but...

It was Virginia.

Her body was cremated to the tune of Dance of the Blessed Spirits, but during a walk with his friend Willie that afternoon Leonard told him he had not liked it because the words did not fit. They had previously agreed they wanted the cavatina from Beethoven's B flat quartet to be played, but he was so overwhelmed by grief that he had not requested it. So he played it at home in the evening when he was alone.

Leonard buried Virginia's ashes under an elm tree in their garden; they had previously named the two elm trees Leonard and Virginia. Leonard's ashes followed under the other elm in due course. One, if not both of the elms are no longer there, due to storms and Dutch Elm disease, but there is a bust of them both in the gardens for visitors to see on their way to Virginia's writing lodge.

Not long before Virginia died a bomb had been dropped in the river, causing a miniature lake that had reached the edge of their garden and which attracted various waterfowl. Returning

German pilots used to jettison their bombs before flying back to base across the English Channel.

The locals knew very little about Virginia although she had lived there for twenty-two years. Gran thought she was known by some as the harmless local madwoman. Others thought she was a brilliant woman who wore expensive hats and wrote books, but nobody they knew had read any of them. They said she was tall and thin, like a bean stick, and wore a long mackintosh. Somebody noticed the great big holes in her stockings. She was thought to be very shy as she usually walked in places where she wouldn't meet people. But another villager's opinion was that Virginia seemed interested in everything and would sometimes stop by a road mender or a carter and talk to them, just as anyone else would. She was a member of and treasurer for the local WI for a while; she gave one or two talks and once put on a play with her literary friends for them. Virginia was a solitary walker and would sometimes walk up to eight miles in the afternoon and other times she would cycle to Lewes and other places. They owned a motor car for longer trips but she also used the village shop and post office.

"You cannot find peace by avoiding life"

After the war both Leonard and my grandmother were getting older so she only popped into Monks House now and again to do some cleaning and return his laundry. I went with her on several occasions when I was staying with her. Do not touch anything Virginia! Especially do not touch any of the books and papers that were lying around. I did get to help Gran sort out the laundry which she would take home to wash, dry and iron. They were flat irons in those days and non-electric. You heated them up on the stove; as you ironed with one, the other one would be heating up and the handles got too hot so you had to hold them with a cloth. Homemade padded squares were made out of scraps of material with a hanging loop stitched into one corner.

"Dashing away with the smoothing iron,
She stole my heart away"

Leonard kept bees in his side garden; they had purchased a neighbouring field from the farmer after Virginia had sold more books. I used to watch him tend them with his one piece coverall and his netted hat on, from Gran's cottage just across the road. He used to puff them with smoke to settle them down first - not from his pipe!

CHAPTER TWO

My first memory in life was falling off my tricycle at the tender age of two, which I still remember because it bloody hurt. I somersaulted over the handlebars when the kerbstone stopped my trike dead. I ended up face down with my nose stuck in a drain grating. It's still there, that offending piece of iron on the corner of Barley Fields road. Luckily the village nurse lived in the cottage across the road, she had her front door open and came running over to rescue me when she heard me hollering and screaming. She carried me into her house where she proceeded to calm me down and clean me up, then put iodine on my cuts and grazes, especially my nose, which *stung*. Then I bawled and yelled some more so she carried me kicking and sobbing to my gran's house which was just up the lane and round the corner. We had a well too, it has been cemented over but the evidence is still there, to the left of the front door of the house now named Bybles.

I was a proper little handful, by all accounts, so much so that one week I slept in my cot in my parents bedroom and the alternate weeks I slept in my gran's room. I say slept but that was the trouble, apparently I didn't do much of that and I cried a lot too. Nothing much has changed since then because I am a veritable night owl and so rather anti-social in the mornings. For instance, it is precisely 2.58 in the morning right now as I write this bit with a smile on my face and Elvis crooning low.

I took the nose dive because I was on my way to meet my father who cycled home from work at the same time every day. I would pedal halfway up the village then sit on the top of a grassy bank (which seemed like a mountain to me) and wait for him to come into sight down The Street from the main road. Although I had the run of the village where everybody knew me and who I belonged to; I knew, even at that young age, I was not allowed any further up the road because the odd motor car or tractor might come swinging round the corner and knock me off my tricycle. As it turned out, I didn't need any help with accidents, I was more than capable of creating my own!

Sometimes my granddad would walk by on his way home from work as a farm labourer in the neighbouring village of Northease. I would hear his brown leather boots topped with matching gaiters clumping down the street and think, "That's my granddad" but I wasn't allowed to speak to him, nor he to me, because he had left my gran for 'that other woman'. Ironically, their rear gardens backed onto each other, but luckily there was a flint stone wall dividing them which they couldn't see over when pegging out their washing or picking the runner beans. I knew nothing of this when I was little, but Gran must have felt dreadfully hurt and I think she was very brave to stay put and carry on as normal, after all it was *her* village, not his.

My granddad was never spoken about in front of me, although I did gather that my dad and his brother went to their father's cremation and his ashes were scattered on Rodmell cricket pitch. After my dad died I asked my mum about him but she knew next to nothing. So after I retired and Mum had died, I found out about him myself by tracing my family tree, because I was still curious. The first thing I did was find out his real forenames, as I only knew him as Jack, which didn't show up in searches, and then I sent for his birth certificate and found his Army records.

One day Gran came home with a funny looking yellow thing in her basket. This, I was told was a banana, the first one I had ever seen. Because of the war all our imports had stopped and everybody was living on rations and home-grown produce.

However, on this day my mum made sandwiches with the banana (which is still my favourite fruit). She cut it into thin slices and carefully arranged them between home baked, hand sliced, thinly buttered bread and added a sparse sprinkling of sugar, then cut it into quarters. My quarters were put on a china plate which I carefully carried out of our cottage - known simply as The Cottage when we lived there - around the corner and over the stile to sit on a grassy bank to eat them. They tasted delicious, the weather was sunny and warm and I remember my very first picnic as if it were only yesterday. The bank is still there, as is the other one up the village street. I always pay them homage whenever I visit Rodmell - and that drain of course. I've still got the wonky conk!

"Yes we have no bananas, we have no bananas today"

There was an annual village flower show with prizes for best vegetables, flowers, fruit and handicrafts. It was held in the village hall which Rodmell resident author Leonard Woolf donated by purchasing an old Army hut from Seaford Camp after the war. Today it has been replaced by a purpose built brick building on the same site, just around the corner from the Old Rectory. Gran used to enter every year as she was a keen gardener and she entered me into some of the children's classes. One of these was to make a miniature garden. I assume we'd had a tin of biscuits for Christmas as I made my garden in a round tin lid. I used my mum's small round make-up mirror for a pond, then arranged the rest of the lid with mud, turf, gravel, bits of hedge, daisies and buttercups. That year I won first prize.

Another annual event was the fancy dress and village fete held in the top field next to the pub. The field is the pub's car park nowadays with some housing on it. One year my gran handmade me a long lilac coloured dress with puff sleeves, complete with poke bonnet and a basketful of lavender from the garden, which she called Lavender Girl. I won second prize; a cowboy won first prize and I guess that was because he was the only boy who entered!

# # # # # # #

Every Spring we picked primroses and violets from the verges and fields. My mum would loosely wrap some in damp newspaper inside a cardboard box and post them off to her mum in London. They must have had a special significance because my dad's love letters to Mum addressed her as "My dearest darling Primrose". How sweet! When I was a teenager I found them in a pretty shoe box at the bottom of her wardrobe and I used to lay in the bath and secretly read them. I made little bunches with some primroses, tied them up with string, looped them onto a stick and took them round the village where the kindly villagers usually gave me sweets in return. That is how I learned to tie my own shoelaces.

We would go down to the Brooks and gather watercress by hooking it out of the flowing stream with the handle end of Gran's walking stick. Back home she would make us egg and watercress sandwiches for tea. The eggs were hard boiled, cooled and sliced and were from our own chickens; she sprinkled a little salt on but the watercress already tasted peppery. It was easier to butter the end of the loaf first before cutting off a slice with a serrated bread knife in a sawing action, as there was no such thing as ready sliced bread in those days. Baking your own bread was a daily event and easy; just mix the dough with the yeast, leave it in the bowl covered with a damp cloth to rise, then knead it into shape and bake it.

In the autumn we walked up Mill Lane and into the fields at the top of Mill Hill where there were blackberry bushes all along the hedgerows, to fill our baskets with the ripe and juicy fruit (okay I ate mine). Then Mum and Gran made blackberry and apple pie for pudding and lots of jars of jam. Some to keep, some to exchange for other fruit jams, and some to sell at the Women's Institute to raise funds. I remember quince, gooseberry and raspberry jams being exchanged, those neighbours only going as far as their gardens to pick their fruit! The apples were a local variety called Beauty of Bath, they were small, striped and sweet. Some villagers left wheelbarrows or trugs full of windfalls outside their houses, free for the taking. That was how village life used to be, make do and mend, give and take. "There is a war on, don't you know!" This tradition still carried on for years after the war ended, thanks to the WI, which is one hundred years old this year.

East Sussex County Council Wartime Cookery Leaflet
Pickles and Chutneys
April 1945

Green Tomato Chutney

4 lb. green tomatoes...........12 red chillies
1 lb. apples..........................1 lb. shallots
1/2 lb. stoned raisins..........1 pint vinegar
1 lb. brown sugar.................1/2 oz. bruised ginger

The tomatoes should be peeled and sliced, placed in a basin with salt between each layer, left for 12 hours and then drained. The apples, shallots and raisins should be chopped and all the ingredients placed in a pan, brought to the boil, and cooked until the chutney has the consistency desired. It should be allowed to cool then put into jars and sealed.

Ripe Tomato Sauce

6 lb. tomatoes......................Spiced vinegar :
1/2 lb. sugar........................1/2 pint vinegar
3/4 oz. salt.........................1/4 oz. cinnamon bark

1/4 oz. paprika......................1/4 oz. whole allspice
1/4 oz. blades of mace........1/4 oz. cloves
Pinch cayenne.......................1 fluid oz. Tarragon or Chilli vinegar

The spices, tied loosely in muslin, should be added to the vinegar, brought to the boil and allowed to infuse for two hours with the lid on the pan. The tomatoes should be full ripe and a good red colour. They should be washed and sliced and then cooked until the skins are fairly free. The pulp should then be rubbed through a hair or metal sieve after which the sugar, salt, cayenne and paprika should be added and the sauce cooked until it begins to thicken. At this stage the spiced vinegar and the tarragon vinegar should be added and the sauce cooked until it is the consistency of thick cream. It should be filled into hot bottles and sealed up at once. If corks are used for sealing they should be previously soaked in hot water.

Pickled Green Tomatoes

3 lb. green tomatoes...............1 lb. Demerara sugar
1 lb. small onions....................1 quart spiced vinegar

The tomatoes and onions should be sliced, sprinkled with salt, left overnight, and drained thoroughly. The sugar and vinegar should be boiled, the tomatoes and onions added and cooked until tender. They should then be put in jars and sealed.

Date Chutney

1 lb. stoned dates......................1/4 oz. salt
1/4 lb. stoned raisins................6 red chillies
1/4 lb. shallots or onions.........1 pint vinegar
1/4 lb. sugar

The dates, raisins and onions should be chopped finely, put in a pan with the other ingredients and boiled until tender. Allow to cool, put in jars and seal.

These are my grandmother's recipes from her wartime leaflet. I have only made the first one myself, when we had a glut of green tomatoes. It was tasty but the colour wasn't very appetising to look at.

# # # # # # #

I learned to knit aged eight in my great-aunt Dorothy's house. It was a bright green bobble hat and the bit I liked best was making the bobble by winding the wool around a circle of card with a hole in the middle. The old milk bottle tops already had a small circle in the centre ready to push out. Every girl learned how to knit, sew and cook back then, either at school, at home or both. Reading was also important and bedtime stories were a must. I had books for my birthdays and a girls annual every Christmas right up until I left school. But I liked my gran's stories best when she read them to me. Hers was the only lap I sat on, nobody else picked me up and cuddled me.

Gran's book was Hans Christian Anderson's illustrated *Fairy Tales and Stories*. Jumping ahead in time a little there are other childhood books I recall. Mum gave me *Little Women* by Louisa M. Alcott and *A Lonely Little Lady*, a lovely old-fashioned story about a girl named Brownie. Dad once presented me with *Consider the Lilies* (children's bible stories). Another book I recall was the special Coronation edition of the Bible which I received for my tenth birthday. Susan Coolidge's *What Katy Did* and *What Katy Did Next* were birthday presents and almost standard birthday and Christmas gifts would be the Cherry Ames Nurse series. These were written by Helen Wells and Julie Tatham who published a whopping twenty seven Cherry Ames Nurse series between 1943 and 1968 with titles like *Cherry Ames: Student Nurse*, *Cherry Ames: Senior Nurse* and *Cherry Ames: Hospital Nurse*. I liked them because Cherry Ames was often smarter than the doctors and worked out problems they could not.

Counting and adding up was easy for me because Gran ran the village shop after the war when the other lady retired. It was attached to the front of our cottage so I was always in and out watching Gran slice off rashers of bacon with a hand slicing machine, cutting out a portion from a large round cheese with a cheese wire; weighing them, and sugar, butter, potatoes or other groceries on the scales where you added little weights until each side balanced.   If I had been a good girl I was allowed to put the takings into rows of the same coin on the floor and then count them up, before my bedtime. I liked that game!

The milk was delivered every day by horse and cart, a by-product of which was the horse manure in the street which Gran ran out to collect with a bucket and shovel to feed her vegetable plot - the original organic gardening. We used to give the garden birds our bacon rinds which they must have thought were worms because they ate them. We had an earth closet in the outhouse which was emptied into the runner bean trench in the Spring before planting. It was turned into compost the rest of the year, to enrich the soil. The farm milkman had a big metal milk churn on the back of his cart, Gran would go out with her china jug or pitcher which he filled up with his ladle and the horse fed from his nose-bag while Milky gave Gran the gossip.

That reminds me of my mother-in-law; she told her milkman off one rainy day for leaving the lid off the churn and letting the rain in; she told him she was not paying full price for watered-down milk. Always after a bargain was my mother-in-law, bless her cotton socks.

To store the milk you had to choose a cool, shady place indoors and keep a muslin net over the top weighted down with beads sewn around the edge, to keep the flies and wasps out, as we had no refrigerator back then. Before fridges people used meat safes, a ventilated metal box on legs kept out of doors where it was cooler. We had a larder cupboard in the kitchen with a stone slab shelf on which to keep the food cool and on which Mum kept a child's ugly, squashy, orangey, plastic toy fish to deter my brothers from sticking their fingers in the food. My brother still shudders at the memory of it!

CHAPTER THREE

All good things come to an end. I do not mean the war which had finally ended with no fatalities in my close family but I do mean my idyllic life in Rodmell.

By the late 1940's we were overcrowded in Gran's house. There was Gran, Dad, Mum, myself and baby brother plus Aunt Josie, Uncle Albert and their two children; so five adults and four children in a three bedroom house. Luckily for us, the Government built a lot of new houses for its returning forces and their families. So all the young parents in Rodmell put their names down on the waiting list. It was pot luck where you were allocated something and ours was a prefab in Ringmer, along with several other Rodmell families who all knew each other, especially the men who had grown up together.

My dad was not a mixer or a socialiser, he was a loner, so once we had moved to Ringmer we were basically on our own. My parents kept themselves to themselves, even though other Rodmell families lived in the same Close. His cousin and family lived next door and his brother and family lived four doors along. Mum made one friend there and sometimes went to the cinema in Lewes with her sister-in-law. On one of those occasions my little brother and I had picked and eaten green strawberries from our garden. No surprise then that we were both sick that evening after being put to bed, when Mum was out and Dad was looking after us. I wasn't the spoiled little Rodmell girl any more, I was supposed to be the responsible elder sister now, so he told me while he cleaned up the mess!

I had to do a lot of looking after Eddy during the day while Mum was busy looking after our baby brother, doing the laundry, cleaning and cooking but I didn't mind as he was a sweet kid.

One Christmas Eve Eddy and I had been put to bed all bathed and excited in the bedroom we shared when I heard sleigh bells. Eddy was asleep so I got up and looked out of the window expecting to see Father Christmas in the sky being pulled along by his reindeers. I couldn't see him though so I reluctantly got back into bed and fell asleep. The next morning I woke Eddy up and we happily spied then ripped open our presents which had been left at the bottom of our beds. Father Christmas had stopped at our house but must have waited until I was asleep. Guess what I unwrapped first? A skipping rope with jingling bells in the handles! My big present was a doll dressed in a set of lovely clothes from underwear to outerwear, which my gran had hand-made. I decided to name her Margaret Elizabeth, after the Queen and her sister. My brother had a blue and white stuffed dog which he named Buntings, he took it to bed every night and I think he still has it. I still have my doll but minus the head because in later years I allowed my daughters to play with her on the doorstep; their friend Carol joined them and my doll got dropped on the concrete, the body was clothed but her head wasn't protected. Such a shame. I used to stuff banana into her rosebud mouth and she could open and shut her blue eyes.

Margaret Elizabeth and Buntings were later to feature in the novel which I co-researched and edited: *Will's War in Brighton.* One of the characters in that book is called Brenda and the story is partially told from her point of view. Brenda has a little brother called Eddie whom she has to look after all the time. Basically, in providing feedback to the experiences of the main character, I revealed how my childhood was different to that of Will and the author sneakily used all of that information to create a whole new character.

The book has since been added to the collection of the Sussex archives at The Keep in Brighton and it brings a little smile to my face to know that Margaret Elizabeth and Buntings have become a part of Sussex history. Who would have thought it?

CHAPTER FOUR

Ringmer was just a rural village in the 1950's when we lived there. Today it has no social housing left, because over the years the council houses were all bought by the occupiers since Prime Minister Margaret Thatcher came into power and gave all council house tenants the Right To Buy their homes in 1980. (We dubbed her *Thatcher the Milk Snatcher* because the Iron Lady took the children's free school milk away).

Unfortunately the money paid by the mortgages went into the Treasury instead of into building more homes so we have a countrywide shortage of affordable housing today. The governments of the day since then have not addressed the problem enough and developers prefer to build more expensive houses to gain more profit, even on greenfield sites if they can get away with it, to the detriment of our countryside, wild animals, birds and rural way of life.

Ringmer house prices are now sky high and lots, if not most, of the residents are incomers. It's another Sussex village they commute from to London; they drive the car to Lewes railway station, jump on the train and are in the City in about an hour. They can work on their laptop, talk or text on their mobiles and hey presto! they have arrived. Making the same commute on their return journey means they get the best of both worlds. London salaries with the countryside to enjoy in the evenings and at weekends. They normally go abroad for their annual holidays. A far cry from when we grew up there and walked everywhere, even to Lewes and back, except for maybe a Sunday afternoon drive, as only some dads had cars back then.

Prefabs were brand new prefabricated two bedroom bungalow type houses shipped in panels and erected on site. They had asbestos in them which is considered dangerous to health these days. They even had a kitchen sink with running water, an electric cooker and water boiler already installed as well as a proper bathroom. They each had a wrap-around garden to cultivate and a shed; our prefabs were grouped in a Close around a central Green and backed onto fields.

I liked living there, it was right out in the country, opposite a farmyard, although it was a long walk to school and back, about two miles each way. However about halfway along Broyle Lane leading up to the main road was a sweet shop. The thought of this kept me able to put one foot in front of the other on the walk home after all day at school. You could buy sweets for one penny, or better still four for a penny if they were Black Jacks or Fruit Salads, sticky chewy squares. The owners were a Mr and Mrs Wiltshire. I used to play with their two daughters while their parents ran the shop and Mr Wiltshire used to play with my aunt because that's where one of my cousins comes from!

On the way home, after leaving the main road and turning into the lane, I had to pass a group of council houses where the school bully Phyllis Hart lived. Sometimes she would get there first and run out into the road when she saw me coming; barring my way by outstretching her arms. I was only eight and had my younger brother Eddy with me, he was only five so I caught hold of his hand and kept on walking, staring straight ahead. I can't explain what it felt like; a bit like trying to walk through a road block, but one skinny girl is all it was! And that's not all, further down the lane round the bend lived fat, smelly, Tony Paget and he did exactly the same thing when he saw me and Eddy coming, lying in wait at his front gate. After a week of this, I decided not to tell tales to my dad who worked all day, or my mum who had our baby brother to look after so I took a sharp right when I saw him there, through a farm gate and dragged Ed all around the fields to get home. Fight or flight - I took the latter way out!

# # # # # # #

The village school was an old Victorian building, not very large and quite a dreary place in which to learn. We stayed at this school from age five to fifteen so we all knew each other and most of us lived near enough to meet up and play out together at weekends and in the school holidays. I had a new baby brother named Andrew by now, so was left to my own devices a lot, which suited me fine because I was used to being a loner at Rodmell. It's not easy being the eldest child and I had no sister to play with.

I did have a best friend called Pat who lived in the same Close, she was an only child so her mum spoiled her; for instance, she got three pennies to spend on sweets to my one penny and she had a two wheeled bicycle before I did. We learned to ride our new bikes around the Green, falling off, picking ourselves up and trying to keep our balance again and again until we got the hang of it. My first two wheeler was a beautiful blue one for my eighth birthday, one August, just right for the summer holidays. I also remember my gran gave me a tin that year which she had decorated and filled with threepenny bits. I was rich! Pat and I used to re-read my old *GIRL* comics stored in Dad's shed away from my little brothers. I got all the weekly editions and the Christmas specials.

The good thing is, the Close and the Green are still there but it has senior citizen's bungalows around it now. Sometimes Pat and I used to take my brother and his friend Chris with us when we went exploring. The fields were flat as Ringmer is not hilly so we loved to roam across the fields, around the lanes and in the *shaws* (a Sussex word for small woods). In those halcyon days we stayed out all day long in the school holidays and only went home when we felt hungry, or one of us fell over and was bleeding, or it was getting dark, whichever happened first.

If we made a mistake and roamed through a field of bullocks thinking they were cows (oh yes we did) and they started following us, we used to panic and sprint to the safety of the nearest shaw which were on the edges of the fields, and stay there until the bullocks lost interest and wandered off. There was always a problem with barbed wire fences as getting through, under or over was a nightmare when you were escaping wild animals, and I still have the scars on my leg to prove it!

The summer holidays were especially idyllic, endless days of unbroken sunshine, or so it seems now, laying on our backs looking up at the clouds slowly scudding by, putting buttercups under each other's chins to see if we liked butter, picking daisies in the wild flower meadows and making daisy chains for our hair, with matching necklaces and bracelets; we were hippies long before they were invented!

One drawback was the cowpats. They were firm on the surface, dried by the sun, but if you trod or even worse, sat on one, not looking where you were going, you got a stinky foot or bum because they were runny underneath. Our mums were not pleased when (not if) you went home looking and smelling like you-know-what, because laundry days were only on a Monday. The washing was hung out to dry on the line after being put through the mangle. If you helped with threading the clothes through while turning the handle you had to be careful not to squash your fingers in the roller; mangling was quite an art. On Wednesdays it was ironed then put away until bath night on Fridays. On Tuesdays and Thursdays Mum went food shopping. That was the routine in our house as the idea was to be clean for the weekends. I'm afraid I was a proper tomboy and a mucky pup; I think I should have been born a boy, which is what my parents wanted for their firstborn anyway.

Washing babies nappies was a daily chore for all mothers. Disposable nappies were not imported to England until I had my fifth baby, so you can imagine how many I had to wash, dry, air and fold, like millions of mums before me. Well rinsed out so baby didn't get nappy rash and you didn't iron nappies because they needed to be soft and fluffy.

Going to Saturday morning pictures at the Odeon in Lewes was the highlight of the week for my brother and I. We went by bus and were given the fare, sixpence admission, and three pence each to spend in Woolworths on sweets to eat in the cinema. They sent us a card for our birthdays which entitled us and a friend to free admission the following Saturday, so Eddy and I shared ours with each other - our mum made us!

We sat in there watching the film once when something kept irritating the back of my head. When I turned around I saw two boys flicking sweet wrappers at me. We soon became friendly which made me look forward to Saturday mornings even more. One was called Roger and his father was the manager of Lewes racecourse. I forget the other one's name, so you can tell which one impressed me the most. Oh, it's on the tip of my pen.......Michael, that's it.

The Sunday school we attended was Ringmer Congregational Chapel, and for her latest birthday, sixty years later, I gave my eldest daughter the book 'Little Women' by Louisa M. Alcott that I had been awarded for good attendance way back in 1955. Most people were real church or chapel people back in the day: Modest, hard-working and churchgoers. A girl I went to school with in Ringmer, called Hannah, had a family which went three times every Sunday, foregoing the traditional roast dinner because of all the services they attended.

When I was nine, after my youngest brother was born, we were given a three bedroom council house still within the village of Ringmer and right opposite the school, much to my delight. No more long walks to and fro to avoid the bullies. I was sad to leave Pat but we would still see each other at school. Although we were best friends we were rivals in sport. I took great satisfaction beating her in the skipping race every year. It was the only event I managed to beat her in as she was always first and I was always second in the flat races, but I was best at high jump and long jump which Pat didn't do. We used to be presented with postal orders as prizes, which could be exchanged at the post office for money.

Dad bought our first television set at this time so Mum could watch the Queen's Coronation; we were only allowed to watch children's hour after school but I remember watching the Coronation in between playing out, it seemed to go on all day so I think we must have been given the day off school. Also, the local landowner, Sir John Christie, held a special garden party in his stately home at Glyndebourne (now a famous opera house). He invited the locals to picnic on his lawns and presented us children with a china Coronation mug each to commemorate the historic event. The other event I vividly remember is being chased by one of his swans after I had wandered off. It rose out of the water and started running towards me with it's whopping great wings flapping wildly propelling it over the grass, so I fled back to Mum.

# # # # # # #

The school canteen was an oblong prefabricated building round the back on the edge of the playing fields. I had to have school dinners, which I remember were sixpence a day. Most of the time they were edible and I queued up for seconds, but Monday dinners were beef stew which I detested, all gristle and fat, ugh! You could be chewing a lump for hours or surreptitiously spit it out into your hand and drop it on the floor. Some puddings were tastier than others; jam tart and custard, if you didn't mind lumpy custard and brick-like pastry, red jelly with pink blancmange was alright after I had given the skin to one of the boys. I liked the skin on the rice pudding though. Another milk pudding we called frog's eyes on account of it being slimy, but I think it's proper name is tapioca. Semolina was nice, with a blob of jam on that you stirred in with your spoon, it tasted creamy and nutty. Which reminds me of a nutty boy named William who used to chase me around the playground calling me 'rhubarb and custard' - only he knows why - or chant this nursery rhyme at me:

"Old Mother Hubbard went to the cupboard
To get her poor doggie a bone,
But when she got there
The cupboard was bare,
So the poor little doggie had none"

I got into trouble once in school when I stole the Dutch boy Nils' fountain pen. I coveted it. I have no idea why, but I took it home and buried it in the front garden underneath my bedroom window. Somehow my dad found out, he must have seen the disturbed earth, or was alerted by the school I suppose, because he took it to the Headmaster, Mr. Hitter. He called me into his office, told me to bend over his lap and caned my bottom, with the head dinner lady sitting in as witness. That wouldn't be allowed these days, but it did me no harm and taught me a lesson. Nils got his pen back and I had a new one for my birthday.

"Thou shalt not steal"

I failed the eleven plus exam to go to Grammar school, which really disappointed me. I should have seen it coming because although I was always top of the class in English subjects, I was usually bottom in Maths, and relegated to the back of the classroom in exasperation by the obnoxious Maths teacher, Mr. Jones. I once had a Maths exam paper where I was unable to answer any of the questions as my mind went blank, so I just sat there while everybody else was scribbling away and for that non-effort I was awarded 0/100!

I largely ignored the other subjects like History and Geography, preferring to look out of the window daydreaming and waiting for the end of lesson bell to ring. Teachers used to rap your knuckles with a wooden ruler if you didn't pay attention in those days, or chuck their chalk at you. More bodily harm! I was good at cookery lessons but didn't enjoy it; I could make a neat Swiss roll and tasty sausage rolls but didn't like the end of term oven cleaning job. I couldn't act, sing or dance, being shy, tone deaf and having two left feet. One year Miss Bliss decided to put on a play with a Dame Durden it. I was initially chosen to be the Dame, but when she found out I couldn't act she banished me to the book corner and gave my part to somebody else!

I had graduated to a bigger bicycle by now. One Christmas after I had opened my presents I was sent to the shed by dad to fetch some sticks to light the fire. On opening the shed door I was surprised to see a bicycle hanging up in there, it was painted a shiny black, but hanging up to dry he explained to me when I went back indoors with the firewood. Beside it was a brand new wicker half-moon shaped basket to attach to the front handlebars with brown leather straps, which my gran had made. And a shiny new bell from my younger brothers. No lights though, because I was not allowed out in the dark. I used to cycle along Norlington Lane to the farm where the chickens were free range, hang around making sure nobody was looking, dip my hands into the hedgerow where I knew the hens laid some eggs, then gingerly ride home with three to five eggs in my basket many a time, and never got caught. Five was a good haul because there were five of us in the family.

Every Fifth of November we celebrated with fireworks due to the Guy Fawkes tradition when he tried to blow up the Houses of Parliament. Dad used to bring home a box of assorted fireworks and after tea we would go outdoors and watch while he let them off one by one, giving us each a sparkler to hold. One year I waved my sparkler about a bit too much, making patterns in the dark, the sparks went into the basket holding the assortment of fireworks and the whole lot went up in one go! Luckily I didn't get told off because it made a nice big but quick display. Another year dad took Eddy and I to Lewes to watch the famous bonfire night procession with fireworks. We were standing about halfway up School Hill watching the procession with lots of people letting off their fireworks, when a spark from somewhere landed on my best coat and burnt a hole in it, right in the front up near the lapel. I was so upset.

Prior to that I had worn my previous new coat to stoolball practice on Ringmer Green. My parents were out so I thought I could risk wearing it and they would never know. I just wanted to show it off even though it was summer. Well, I did that alright! I'd hung it on a post to play stoolball and when it was time to go home I forgot about it. After I arrived home I remembered it and ran back to fetch it. But it had gone.

Vanished.

Disappeared.

I had to go back home and explain this to my parents. Dad came back with me to see if he could find it but what he did see was the Fair on the other side of the green. No point in looking for it anymore. He glared over at them and a group of women just stared back at us. I had to wear a second-hand coat that winter which my gran found in a Jumble Sale. It was green, the same colour as my new shoes I ruined by spilling pale blue paint on in the garage after we had moved to Newhaven. I will let you into a secret now, I spilled the paint on my shoes on purpose because I didn't like wearing them as I thought they made my size eight feet look too big. They were brogue lace-ups. My parents kitted me out for practicality and comfort, not fashion!

#######

I reached the age of eleven in Ringmer when my life turned sour. Worse than somebody stealing my coat and worse than being caned at school. Mum used to go to the hairdressers in Lewes once a week which happened to be the same day as the laundry man delivered and collected our laundry, (she sent the white cotton sheets and pillowcases). I had to go home from school to mind my two younger brothers and wait in for the laundry man until my mother arrived back home, because my father was at work. The delivery/collection was supposed to happen just inside the kitchen door which was kept locked. He was supposed to knock, I was supposed to open the door and stand there until he had put the clean laundry wrapped in brown paper and tied with string, down onto the floor and picked up the dirty laundry also tied with string, from the same place without entering the kitchen. Mum always put the laundry ready in the same spot. Then I just had to sign the receipt book. No money was involved.

For some reason he started coming right into the kitchen, it may have been to borrow a pen, or to lean on the side to countersign the book. I don't know why.

After weighing up the situation a few times he must have figured out my mother was out and my brothers were in the other room watching children's television. After a while he started lifting me up from under my arms so that I was sat on the kitchen side, then he put his hands inside my school top, up and over my budding breasts, down to my knees, then up my legs and inside my navy blue school knickers. He stood there for a while, leaning against me with his hands crawling all over me inside my knickers while looking out of the window; then he finally turned and walked out of the door and into the firm's van which was parked outside. It seemed ages until he finally drove off and I stayed sitting there until he had definitely driven away. This happened week after week. Nothing more but nothing less. I never knew the bastard's name and can't remember the name of the laundry firm but it's van was green and cream. I kept it to myself and told nobody.

Until... I told my husband a long time after I was married. News would come on the television which reminded me of it, most recently the infamous Jimmy Saville revelations. It is a great pity that he died before he was named, shamed, taken to Court and put in prison. No wonder his family quickly removed his fancy black headstone. He used to publicly call his mother the Duchess, all the while molesting girls. It makes me feel sick and angry to know that men get away with these things. I sincerely hope that my grand-daughters have more sense than I had as unfortunately I was too naive and had not been warned about such things.

My husband was understanding and sympathetic, not least because the stories he used to tell me about his childhood were worse than mine anyway, so we had a lot in common. I finally told my mother when we went to visit her once but not until after my father had died.

She said, "Why on earth didn't you tell your dad?"

I remember thinking, 'yeah right' but had no explanation except that I thought it was my fault in some way, that I was somehow to blame, but mainly that I was too *scared* to tell him. The sad thing is, mum didn't respond to my revelation, even though I told her in front of my husband. She was like that, not maternal, no hugs or kisses from her or my dad. So what you've never had, you find hard to give and that is a lonely place to be when you crave for some show of affection.

#######

Fortunately, our parents informed us that we would be moving to Newhaven. They had bought a newly built house on Mount Pleasant which was plenty of miles away from Ringmer. One Friday after school, my brother and I stood at the bus stop outside the school and queued up with the teachers to catch the bus to Lewes bus station then another one to Newhaven. I could see the removal men loading up the van during the day from my classroom window, so I scratched my name deep into the desk then coloured it in with ink. My next lesson was cookery, but a boy was sent to fetch me to go back into the classroom and scrub the desk clean, with a bowl of water and scrubbing brush from the cookery class, so everybody in two classrooms knew about it. Feeling chastised, humiliated and embarrassed, I was never so happy as when I was on that bus to our new house and new life, leaving the village, but not its memories, behind forever.

The day we moved out of Ringmer is the day I left my childhood behind even though I had my first kiss there. No big deal and his idea not mine. It was more of an experiment on the footpath opposite the school. His name was Raymond, his parents were friends with my parents and they were visiting us from Brighton for the day. We went for a walk while they talked, that is all. We went to the pictures one afternoon in Lewes too, but I didn't fancy him, didn't even like him much to tell the truth. He kept trying to hold my hand but I kept pulling it away and putting it in my pocket. Oh, and I managed to accidentally on purpose break his balsawood aeroplane which was stored in my bedroom cupboard because it was in my way as I used the bottom shelf for my desk.

CHAPTER FIVE

Sport is like Marmite, you either love it or hate it. I hate football, especially on television. My husband used to call it overgrown men kicking a bag of wind about, but he liked watching Rugby. I can't see the difference myself! I have enjoyed watching horse racing, mostly on television but sometimes at Newton Abbot racecourse, ever since I won a bet on the Grand National back in 1961. Mum and I watched the runners and riders on the television then she went in dad's office to telephone and put our bets onto his bookies account.

My horse was called Nicholas Silver, a grey, which is why I chose it. He came in at thirty three to one, so with my one pound bet I had enough winnings to pay for a European air/coach tour holiday to Steinach-am-Brenner in the Austrian Tyrol.

My mother had already booked to go on the September holiday with the Lewes Camera Club, where dad was a member, so I was now able to go with her. I remember a lovely chair lift ride up the side of a mountain, and cows with big bells clanging round their necks in the meadow below. I later became pen friends with Jakob, the nice Austrian boy I met in the Kuh

Bar, oh and the Belgian coach driver, Albert, fancied my mum!

My dad rang the hotel every evening to check on us. I also saw the Edelweiss, Austria's national flower, growing in their natural habitat. We drove up and over the Brenner Pass in the coach. At the summit Albert 'pulled the plug' to let the on-board toilet empty, laughingly telling us all to turn round and watch the traffic crawling uphill behind get the deluge! We had a day trip to Innsbruck where we saw the Olympic ski slope and the famous Golden Roof house which shone in the sun, passing two oddly named villages, Mutters and Natters, en route.

On the way home our coach pulled up by the Berlin Wall, which has now been demolished but it had not long been built to divide East and West Germany when we were there. An East German soldier with a gun came on the coach and stared at each one of us in turn while slowly marching the length of it, demanding to see random passports. Scary! Even though we had been warned to have our passports ready and to sit quietly and say nothing.

My first trip abroad was by my one and only aeroplane flight, it was so long ago that the plane had a propeller! My daughter flew on Concorde and even that is obsolete now. Mum went to Europe on holiday with her sister every September after that first foreign holiday, and my father went to Austria and Switzerland to ski with friends every January, when his work was slack. He used to bring us tourist presents back. One year he came through customs with a travel rug draped over his left arm. It turned out this was to conceal a whole armful of Swiss watches he had bought for our family because he didn't want customs to see them with regard to tax. My watch had a white leather strap and I still have my collection of postcards from those days.

I have been to Austria twice since then; the next time was on a Lyons coach tour to Zurs-am-Arlberg with a friend Geoff, whom I met through work and ditched as soon as we got there! I still have a Valentine's card he sent me; he went to London and became a window dresser in a top London store, having studied at Art College. These days he runs a musical theatre company in Sussex, but he wasn't my cup of tea. We went to each other's houses and a few dances together, had a few snogs and then the holiday but that was it. My parents liked him but he wasn't exciting enough for me!

"Distorted realities have always been my cup of tea"

We had various day trips on this holiday, one was to Kitzbuhel where dad had been skiing. I usually preferred to go exploring on my own but one evening I met up with three girls on holiday from Manchester and four German boys working locally. We sort of paired off at the end of the evening and I did not go back to my hotel room. I remember a caravan in a field with bunk beds and hay filled sacks as mattresses and the next morning climbing up a mountain to admire the view with Gerhard.

We could not speak each other's language, which was great fun, I kept repeating, *"Tasche"* which as far as I knew was German for 'bag' because I wanted my cigarettes out of my handbag. When I arrived back at my hotel in time for breakfast, I got dirty looks from the chambermaids in the corridor, who had already been in to clean my room and found that my bed hadn't been slept in, or maybe that was just my guilty conscience!

This particular holiday had been booked while I had been hankering after my friend Helen's brother but getting nowhere with him. I was working in a surgery at the time and that really opened up my eyes because one of my jobs was to dispense packets of three to some of the patients. I decided to put a packet in my bag ready for my holiday. A case of my Girl Guides motto, "Be Prepared?" I don't know, wishful thinking maybe! But I went all the way with Gerhard that night in the caravan in the field in Austria and again next morning up on top of the mountain. Then walked back to my hotel with my undies in my bag and never saw him again. This interaction was no big deal, or so it seemed to me, but the boys liked it, obviously.

My third time abroad my husband and I travelled on another European coach tour in the 1980s. After the ferry crossing we drove through the night to Gotzens in the Austrian Tyrol via France and Germany on the autobahn. Looking out of the coach window I kept thinking it was a long way to *Ausgang* which was on all the signs! Chris overdosed on duty free whisky, had hallucinations on the coach, finally fell asleep then puked up in our room's waste paper bin after we arrived at our hotel. Our room was on the fourth floor with no lift but it had a lovely mountain view. He fell asleep again so I went downstairs for a coffee and a long walk, not returning until hotel dinner time because I was feeling humiliated. We were put on a table of four with a mother and middle-aged daughter who chatted to him as if nothing had happened when he went mad on the coach. At a rest stop in the middle of the night somewhere in Germany, the two drivers said I could get back on but he couldn't. Eventually they relented when he promised to sleep it off. Scary times!

I vowed I would never go abroad with him again but in the early 2000s we went to Brittany in France with our pregnant married daughter, about ten of us in cars via the overnight ferry. I wasn't very impressed with Brittany, where we were staying was very agricultural but we did see some amazing chateaux. Joanna needed to pee badly, we walked around a village but couldn't find a public convenience so I knocked on the door of a local cottage and in extremely limited French with a lot of hand gestures I asked if she could use their toilet.

"Twarlet, bebe, bebe, si voo play?" said I rubbing my stomach and crossing my legs. The rest hovered at the front gate. Luckily the old lady took pity on us and allowed my daughter into her house, while her husband guarded the front door. Problem solved!

The trip I went on with Chris also took in Salzburg, where the film *The Sound of Music* was made and interestingly it was also Mozart's birthplace. We sat in Mozart cafe in Mozart Square drinking coffee so strong you could stand the spoon up in it, admiring the horse statues around the water fountain feature. There was a castle on the hill and the Russian Embassy on the edge of town where a Russian soldier with a furry Cossack style hat on was marching up and down along the frontage carrying a gun.

The coach also took us up a long winding road to Berchtesgaden where Hitler had his Eagle's Nest perched on top of the mountain. The coaches parked where all his soldiers used to live but the way to his house at the top was roped off. *Verboten!* No soldiers about, just tourists like us. I found it difficult to imagine that less than twenty years earlier it must have been a hive of activity with grey uniformed troops goose stepping in their jackboots, with extended arm salute shouting *Heil Hitler*, because it was so peaceful and picturesque when we were there.

#######

Back to sport.

When I was young the game of football was only played in the winter to keep warm. George Best in his 1970s short shorts or further back Stanley Matthews in his long baggy shorts. Georgie was in glorious technicolour and Stanley in black and white; he was knighted for his contribution to the beautiful game (according to some!).

Cricket is our summer game in England, which I think we invented. I have some lovely memories of this game. My grandfather was the umpire for Rodmell Cricket Club. He did play when he was younger but when he was the umpire my dad, his brother and their cousin, all Rodmell lads, played for the team. It was a real family outing to go and watch them, we would take a rug and a picnic to away matches and of course the sun was always shining!

A special memory of the home matches is when my gran was the tea-lady. She lived at the bottom of Rodmell in the first of the row of four cottages (the old Workhouse), which was opposite the gate to the field leading up to the village cricket pitch. In the 1960s after Gran died, planners allowed somebody to convert her modest two bedroomed cottage into a bigger house, which to me is an eyesore and has ruined my memories of staying there. My gran was a determined woman and not going to fade into the distance so she kept control of the big copper tea urn, which we would carry up to the cricket field together and into the pavilion, where she was in charge of the tea and sandwiches. She had a good view of my estranged granddad and the home matches from inside the pavilion, while I preferred to be just outside watching the scorer flipping over the metal score plates. There was an Army pillbox still standing in the corner of the field, left over from the war, which the village boys used to play games in but they also peed in it. The pillbox is still there.

At school I was tall and well built but not fat, although I thought I was; but looking back at my old photo's I can see that I wasn't. I was usually chosen to play in the school sports teams. I was goal defence in netball at Ringmer because I could jump up high enough to knock the ball away when the other side was trying to shoot the ball in the net to score a goal. I was the bully-off girl in hockey at Newhaven, (don't forget your shin pads or you'd limp for a week). It was great fun charging around Newhaven recreation ground in a short PE skirt on a cold day. Yes, really it was, because it got me out of the classroom and I enjoyed being out of doors. Newhaven recreation ground is near the end of the harbour down by the sea and a chilly, windy place to be in the winter, which stood me in good stead for living here by Babbacombe Downs. A hockey rule is never allow your stick to go higher than your shoulders. I had quite a bit of trouble keeping that rule, I have to say! I was a clumsy teenager, my mum used to say I was like 'a bull in a china shop'. Nothing much changes, I still keep breaking things.

In the summer I was in the school stoolball team at Ringmer, we played the inter-school matches on the village green with quite an audience, and embarrassingly I was also in the

Maypole dancing team on the green unfortunately, but with my two left feet I wasn't keen on an audience for that, especially my two giggling younger brothers.

Stoolball is a game peculiar to Sussex, it consists of a wooden square board on a wood post, an all-wood bat shaped like a table tennis bat, and a leather covered ball, like a cricket ball but smaller. It could be a dangerous game but very satisfying to hit the ball hard, hear the 'clonk' and see it flying off, hopefully to the edge of the green, while making as many runs as possible between the two posts before the other side threw the ball back to base; much like cricket.

In Newhaven we lived on Mount Pleasant but when we weren't in school our playground was Denton village. Here I participated in several sports not associated with school, like kiss-chase and tennis. The Girl Guide hut was in Denton recreation ground and the Boy Scouts would be waiting to go in when us Girl Guides came out, so that was kiss-chase time. Tennis was knock-about fun in the Rector's garden, he kindly got someone to mark out a tennis court for us youth club members that was too close to the trees and Mrs Rector's flower beds but we spent many a summer evening playing singles, doubles and mixed doubles. The gardener's step ladder doubled as the umpire's lofty seat, the boys took it in turns to be the umpire while the girly girls sat on the lawn in their full skirts and net petticoats and the other girls happily ran around perspiring trying to win their game. Guess which group I was in?

I was so proud of my second hand racquet that I wouldn't lend it out, not a very nice attitude for a Girl Guide to have but I loved that racquet. Before that, I was a shy little Brownie at Ringmer and after that I was a Cadet for a while, attached to the Denton Guides as a helper to the young ones. As a Guide, I went camping two or three times, a week in a tent in a field, cooking over the campfire, making useful things with sticks, like a tripod for the washing-up bowl, went tracking, played field games and in the evening singing around the fire. My favourite campfire song was *The Quartermaster's Stores.*

The idea was that everyone who sat round the fire took a turn singing a sentence and if you couldn't think of a rhyme for a fellow campers name you could revert back to food items. We sang it as a round and it could go on for a long time until we all ran out of ideas, which was great fun.

At our Youth Club tennis tournaments we had a competition where the winning boy and girl could walk home together at the end of the evening, if they wanted to. I am sure everybody reading this remembers their first proper kiss, well mine was during this summer, his name was Brian and it happened in front of the garage door at home.

I remember it for the circumstances rather than the lip action. He walked me home after we won the mixed doubles. He gave me a goodnight kiss at the top of the drive which tasted nice so we went down the drive to snog in front of the garage door. I had my arms around his neck as he was taller than me and I had to reach up. At this crucial time I dropped my racquet which I was still holding, it clattered to the ground making a loud din in the night air. Then I noticed Mr Drew our neighbour staring at us out of his bedroom window and I was scared that the noise would have woken my dad up too, so the moment was spoiled and the enjoyment was gone. I quickly drew back and Brian had to walk away.

Mr Drew was also my optician and I used to knock on his door asking him to mend my glasses because it was quicker than going to his shop in town. Now I was embarrassed that he had seen me kissing a boy so that put me off future liaisons so close to home. My dad already embarrassed me by being the only father to take the dog for a walk to coincide when we came out of Guides. He would hover in the field and watch us inter-act with the

Scouts who were waiting to go in. I knew I couldn't linger like my friends did, I had to walk home with dad and the dog. Was it caring that he brought Tessa to meet me or was he being over-protective? I don't know, but I do know that I felt curtailed and upset, because I wanted to mix with the boys.

Even now I hate that my dad didn't trust me when I was a young teenager wanting to have innocent fun with my friends. When I was an older teenager he trusted me even less and I lived up to that expectation, I am afraid to say. Dad came out looking for me when he realised I was having lifts home from work; I would see him and Tessa walking towards us parked up in the van and knew I had to get out and accompany him home without a kiss goodbye. I feel sad typing this, it brings back the hurt I felt. There was a distinct lack of communication in our house when I was growing up. If only Mum or Dad or both had sat me down and talked to me about the birds and the bees and more importantly, about feelings. When I was fifteen Mum said she wouldn't need to tell me about the facts of life because she thought I knew more than she did. In actual fact I knew nothing so I asked my friend Brenda at school who told me what she knew, which was a lot and I was shocked.

My father decided to buy a horse, Sherry, as he liked to go hunting with the Southdown Hunt. It is not pc now but it wasn't frowned upon back then. Foxes had to be kept under control as they killed chickens and didn't always eat their kill. Dad built a stables in Denton where the industrial estate is today. He also kept his friend and accountant's horse there in livery which helped him pay the bills. After a while he bought a pony for the local children to have riding lessons, and employed a girl groom called Jenny, who lodged with Brian's parents practically next door to the stables. Sometimes it's not what you know, it's who you know!

One Spring Bank Holiday I had the day off work and decided to go for a ride with Jenny over the Downs. I had never sat on a horse before, nor had any lessons, but had been down the yard after work, mucking out, so I wanted to go with her while she was riding Sherry out. We tacked up and she made it look so easy mounting and sitting up there on the big hunter. So I climbed into the saddle and off we trotted. If you can't rise to the trot (and I couldn't) you are like a sack of spuds atop a horse. This pony called Rusty wasn't rusty at all, but he certainly knew I was, because as soon as we hit the open spaces on the Downs, he bolted. I could do nothing but try to stay on board. I couldn't steer him between all the families walking about, nor pull him up nor have any control over him whatsoever.

I hung on terrified until he ran out of steam, he slowed down and finally stopped. I jumped off, shaking all over, but still holding the reins while Rusty nonchalantly ate grass. Jenny caught me up and said, "It's like riding a bike, you fall off, you get back on." Erm no! I hadn't fallen off and I wasn't getting back on. So I walked Rusty all the way back to the yard escorted by Jenny on Sherry. At least I didn't let go of the beast, because if I had my dad would probably have killed me. I never tried riding horses again and can't even go in the same field unaccompanied where my daughter's horse is kept. I can't drive a car either, having failed my driving test three times, although I've always believed I could drive anywhere so long as nothing else was on the road at the same time. But I've never had the opportunity to try that out!

Now my thoughts turn to the time I was given a Lambretta scooter for my birthday. Dad bought it second-hand from someone in Lewes, in the days before the Mods and Rockers. I was neither of those anyway as he was trying to get me mobile after my unsuccessful attempts to ride a horse or drive a car - I put his Landrover in a ditch once when he let me take the wheel and all the family had to get out while he drove it onto terra firma again. End of that lesson! We kept the scooter parked up in his stables which was a short walk from Mount Pleasant. He tried to teach me a few times after work, up and down the lane by the side of his yard. Balance okay. Clutch control okay. Riding along okay. But the lane was a dead end which required a turn. Every time I tried to turn this great-big-heavy-green-monster around I ended up in the ditch underneath the barbed wire fence. Stuck. With the scooter on its side, engine running and wheels whirring. Dad had to keep walking about a hundred yards to extricate me from the fence and turn off and upright the scooter. I don't remember who lost patience first but we were both tired after work at every lesson, so the scooter was put away and locked up in the stables.

At the Youth Club I casually mentioned that I had a Lambretta. All the boys and half the girls wanted to see it. So we arranged to meet up the next evening and I proudly wheeled it out, enjoying being the centre of attention. Yes, I know it was my scooter and not me they were admiring! After that, the boys used to take turns driving it up and down Heighton hill while I either watched or had a pillion with Brian, wrapping my arms tightly around his waist. No crash helmets were required by law.

Life was good.

Until... I don't know how dad found out but he did and put a stop to it. Looking back I must have not parked it up in exactly the same place I suppose. He sold my scooter because I couldn't ride it and I didn't get a replacement birthday present. To this day my usual form of transport is Shanks' Pony or catch a bus.

########

It was the routine in our house that dad went out for a drink with his friends on Friday nights and he took mum out for a meal on Saturday nights. Muggins here had to babysit my two younger brothers every Saturday night, even when I was working and even when I had to leave the coffee-bar in Peacehaven with its Jukebox to catch the bus home in time to babysit. I didn't mind too much because I thought my mum deserved a treat once a week and because I could put my brothers to bed then get stuck into the chocolate biscuits that were always in the larder, whilst watching the telly. No questions were ever asked about missing packets of biscuits but my dad always put his hand on the television set when they came home to find it still warm, as I'd only turned it off and ran upstairs when I heard the car pull into the garage. He'd call up the stairs, "I know you've only just gone to bed young lady". Well, what do you expect, I thought, but kept quiet and practised my pretend snoring.

CHAPTER SIX

The following seven years of my life were an emotional rollercoaster; I wouldn't have been a normal teenager if they weren't but the trouble was teenagers were not recognised as such back in the 1950s. We were young models of our mothers and fathers, in my case my mum. However my genes did not dictate that I took after her, Mum being a gentle and refined lady, so I had a difficult time being understood. I knew what I wanted but they didn't so there were too many strict rules for me to try to adhere to. I wanted to be loved and praised not molested and ignored. My gran tried to talk to my dad and my aunt tried to talk to my mum about it, but nothing changed, so I guess they couldn't manage the nurturing mode. I also wanted to do well at school and this second want I achieved to my satisfaction. The school leaving age was fifteen in those days but Newhaven County Secondary School had the foresight to select promising pupils to stay on an extra year to study certain subjects and sit national exams.

Fab! I was one of the chosen few and felt honoured. My father agreed to keep me for another year, instead of my having to leave school and get a job with no qualifications in the local Parker Pen factory or similar, which most of my classmates did. I enjoyed my final year at school, our group were all made prefects and were called the fifth year commercial class. We felt grown-up and special and did not have to wear school uniform anymore so we invented our own fashions. One was to wear our dad's socks as knee-highs and we all bought a fashionable bucket bag instead of our old school satchel. Mine was tan coloured plastic as we couldn't afford leather, until Mum bought me a fancy brown leather one back from her holiday in Italy, then the original one became my knitting bag at home. Mum didn't like anything left lying around, all my school books had to be kept in a neat and tidy pile in Dad's office with my reading books in my bedroom. My uncle made me a bookcase which fitted under the window and my doll sat on the chair beside it. My flouncy net petticoat hung in the corner above my bed and my jewellery hung on the mirror of my dressing table. I loved my room.

That winter my dad bought me a black duffle coat, complete with hood and toggles, so I felt like a real student and loved it, swinging down the Drove with the Grammar school boys from the Mount where we all lived. They caught the train to Lewes then my solitary journey on to my school took me along the harbour side past where the caretaker's son drowned in the mud hole, across the road by the recreation ground and up Gibbon road, which took me about half an hour. I carried my knitting and a library book as well as my course work in my bag because we even had free periods when we could sit around and talk, knit, read or revise.

I fainted in the school hall in morning assembly once; when I came to my legs were being carried by the head boy and my shoulders by a male teacher. They dumped me in the needlework room where a lady teacher attended to my menstruation needs. I was fine but embarrassed and used to blush at everything as a teenager. I wore my straight mousey brown hair in a ponytail, put blue eyeshadow over my blue-grey eyes and powder on my spotty, freckled face, with a pale pink lipstick my new best friend Brenda had given me from her collection of Woolworths make-up.

I worked in Seaford Woolworths during the summer holidays, got put on the nails and screws counter where I had to weigh them up to order, take the money and give the change. My friend was put on the sweets counter! I was at the back of the store and she was at the front and we both had to wear the uniform overalls so I decided then that my career would not be in shop work, nor factory work either.

One of the Grammar school boys, Martin, became a famous left-handed guitar player, he played for the Everly Brothers and Barbara Dixon amongst others. His interest in music started when we used to go to his house, or his girlfriend Sandra's house to listen to records on the record player that Dad bought Mum and I was allowed to take to their houses, that was a labour of love as it was a heavy thing to carry. Sandra's parents were very good at letting us teenagers use their front room but everyone was too scared of my dad to come knocking on our door. Martin had a younger brother Gary and they started up a local band, Sandra's brother Geoff was also in it. Martin emigrated to Australia and unfortunately died there; Sandy is gone too but Geoff lives in Italy. Martin's nickname for me was Owlie on account of my glasses. He won a chalk owl for me at the fairground on the Drove field one summer back when fairground rides were sixpence a go. My half-a-crown pocket money (five x sixpence) could buy me four rides and a candy floss or a toffee apple.

In the summer of 1959 I proudly left school with three GCE O levels; English Language, English Literature and Needlework, having failed only one, Religious Knowledge. That was because the subject was too broad and we had not studied the right parts for the set questions, so our tutor said that was his fault. We were taken to the theatre in Brighton to see Macbeth for our literature and a shop in Seaford to choose material for our needlework exam. I wore the dress I made and ripped it under the arm so took it over to my gran in Rodmell where she patched it for me and it still passed! I have the distinction of being the only one to pass the English Language GCE, none of the others passed it that first year, only me! I also passed several RSA's in Typewriting, Pitman's Shorthand, Business Studies, Commerce and more English. I used to get marked 10/10 and comments such as: 'Good attempt at the satirical style' for my essays but I am back to mainly index finger typewriting these days and have forgotten most shorthand.

That was a good age and I remember I bought the record *Only Sixteen* sung by Craig Douglas because of the words as I was sixteen too. Today, one of my granddaughters turned sixteen, how cool is that?

# # # # # # #

Now it was time to look for a proper job. My father said I could spend what would have been the school holidays looking for one. He brought home the local Evening Argus newspaper every day for me to read, sitting in his self-built office at the back of the garage, where I had previously spent many hours doing my homework and revising. I also started typing his business letters for him as he was a self-employed builder and a good one; for instance he would use 4"x3" instead of 3"x2" thickness for his wood supports.

I joined the local library now I had more time to spare, my childhood books and annuals were safely stored away, and because Gran had regaled me with stories about Virginia Woolf living in the village and her connection with our family, I decided to read her books and do a bit of writing myself now that school and exams were behind me. My first story was called 'Lavender's Lost Love' and I had a go at writing about a Welsh boy named Daffyd; I wrote poems too. I had memorised lots for my English exams and still have old hand-written copies of those I liked the best.

"Tiger, tiger burning bright, in the forests of the night"

The more I read Virginia's books, the more interested in her I became, so I borrowed some non-fiction about her. She fascinated me as a person, not only because she used to live just up the road from Gran or because I admired her intellect and ability with words, I also thought we had a lot in common: we had the same name; she smoked, I smoked; neither of us were fussy or fashion conscious, both had minds of our own; both liked going for solitary walks; both got monthly debilitating migraines and neither of us thought we were attractive. I wished I had known her. In later life I also had depression in common with Virginia but unlike her, I managed to beat mine, having learned at a young age it is sink or swim in this life and what doesn't get you down, makes you stronger. I think Virginia's husband Leonard was very supportive and caring towards her, she herself knew she was lucky to have him. If the second world war hadn't happened maybe she would have survived into old age like he did. I think she spent too much time inside her own head. I know from experience this is not good for you. Her diaries, which I have read since becoming an adult, show Virginia to be a troubled woman, trying to concentrate on her writing whilst having a busy life with varied people in it, both in London and latterly in Rodmell, where unfortunately she still did not find peace of mind.

Thoughts of her and my grandmother help to keep me strong during my own journey through life. Throughout my teenage years I tried to remember this quote.

"Growing up is losing some illusions in order to acquire others"

#######

I found a job in the paper that I fancied, telephoned to make an appointment and Dad drove me to the interview in Seaford. While he waited outside, I had my first ever interview and got the job! It was a piece of cake to get a job back then but I think my certificates must have swung it.

Wendy, the girl who was leaving was unmarried but pregnant so they needed a replacement and they chose me. Well, Miss Allenby did. She was the Head Receptionist and I was now the junior receptionist at the doctors' surgery, a practice of six GPs, in East Albany Road, Seaford.

How I loved that job. Being a Virgo I like being of service to others, which incidentally, stood me in good stead when I was married with five children - but that is another story. I liked the routine, the paperwork, the filing, the PBX switchboard, the appointment system, the emergencies, everything about it, especially the patients. I was the flower arranger, the prescription writer, the sample tester, the cover secretary when Joan was off ill or on holiday, and a myriad of other jobs including holding babies when they were being circumcised because their mums couldn't bear to. Call Virginia in, she will do it. I would do anything for anybody, that was me, such a shame it wasn't reciprocated most of the time in my private life.

########

However, one Saturday night things did not go according to plan. I had pulled my back on duty at the surgery that afternoon, by over-reaching to the top shelf to put the files away as I always liked to leave a tidy office. My back hurt so bad I borrowed Dr Smith's chair cushion to sit on and wait for the time I could go home. He popped in for some reason and went into his surgery. The next thing I knew he came into the office annoyed until I explained about my back. Then he let me go home early.

In due course Mum and Dad went out leaving me to babysit as usual. I put my brothers to bed and the television on as normal. My back was hurting worse now so I thought I would lie on the floor to watch TV. Then I discovered I couldn't get up. I couldn't move because of the excruciating pain, so I just had to lay there. Eventually my parents came home and Mum nearly tripped over me on the floor. They got me off the floor, helped me up the stairs and she phoned the doctor. Dr Smith was on duty but he would not come out that night and told Mum to ring again after 8am if the pain had not eased. It didn't so she rang the surgery again, this time it was Dr Crane, he came to see me and by 10am I was being taken to the hospital in Eastbourne by ambulance. They carried me down the stairs in a wheelchair, how I wished I could have stayed downstairs all night. I have never known pain like it, even childbirth didn't seem as bad in future years because I knew that pain would stop, but this pain didn't let up at all.

I was in hospital for six weeks lying flat on my back in the corner bed of the geriatric ward and I was only sixteen. Some of the old dears would come and talk to me, some of the nurses would eat my chocolates, some friends visited me as did Dr Crane. Mum came by bus every Wednesday and my dad, brothers and mum came every Sunday afternoon. I had lots of cards and chocolates so life wasn't too bad. A fellow patient, Betty, used to give me some of her treats as well. After six weeks the doctors decided I could get out of bed because the pain had finally gone. They called it a red herring but I think it was a slipped disc. To learn to balance and walk again I had to have physiotherapy by the side of the bed. I went home in time for Easter and spent another month convalescing in the garden. The surgery had got a replacement receptionist to stand in for me and although they were understanding and held my job open for me, I decided not to go back there. Mainly because I wanted a change and my parents wanted me to become a librarian.

"Each has his past shut in him like the leaves of a book known to him by heart and his friends can only read the title"

While convalescing, I applied for a job at the County Library Headquarters in Lewes, went for the interview and got the job. Again, qualifications counted. The pay was almost twice what it had been at the surgery but the work was boring. I caught the bus to work which took nearly an hour, then sat on the top floor in the specialised books department typing out book tickets all day long, only seeing one or two old men and Doreen, the other typist, who introduced me to Du Maurier cigarettes and cigarette holders. So I bought one and felt like Princess Margaret using it.

After six months I'd had enough and handed in my notice, because meanwhile I was head-hunted at the bus stop by Gillian, who also lived on Mount Pleasant and was working at the surgery in my old job. There was a vacancy and Miss Allenby wanted me to go back, so I did, back to my old job, senior to Gill and with new pay that matched the library rates. Soon after that, Gillian left as she decided she did not like the evening shifts. Anita was taken on but she didn't last long either. Gill and I still keep in touch and she married Brian from the youth club!

########

When I started work at the surgery I bought myself a monthly bus pass to travel to work and back and found out I could use it in the evenings as well, so this led me to new friends and my first proper boyfriend with whom I fell madly in love. I loved him for four years but the trouble was, he didn't really love me back, he used me for sure, but that's not the same thing. He was the older brother of Helen, a new friend who became a good friend, she worked in the local library and we spent a lot of time off work together. His name was David, he was twelve years older than me and going through a divorce, although I didn't know it at the time.

He later told me that his wife Sarah had gone off with her boss, she was a secretary at EMI records. My dad probably didn't approve because of the age gap so David only came to our house once. We were playing records in the front room with his sister. My mum brought in a tray of tea and biscuits to meet him and she must have given my dad her opinion because I was told I shouldn't see him again. He lived in a flat in Berkshire and was a teacher in a boys boarding school there. He came down some weekends to stay with his parents in Seaford so

I engineered that I could stay with Helen at the same time. Helen and I would sleep in their garden caravan.

Well, I promised the truth come what may. I lost my virginity to a Jewish lad named Aaron, I was only sixteen and so was he. They are circumcised you know, and I already knew what that meant by working in the doctor's surgery and holding the boy babies for their nervous mums. He lived in a big house opposite a caravan which was home to one of my friends called Angie. Aaron used to come over and hang around in the evenings. One evening Angie told me she had 'done it' with him because he wanted to be initiated and he had asked her to ask me if I would 'do it' with him too. I agreed because I was curious as well. So Angie and her boyfriend Bob went out for a walk, even though it was raining as I recall, and we 'did it' standing up. So unemotional and unimpressive I thought; he wasn't impressed either because he later told Angie who bragged to me that she was the best one. So let them get on with it, I decided, and promptly forgot all about it.

David continued to be far more interesting. We had fun driving around in his car he called 'Polly Anything' with Helen and her boyfriend John, going for hikes, playing tennis in Seaford, canoeing down the Cuckmere river and generally just hanging out together. His cat was called 'Itmog' and I was stupid enough to ask why so he replied, "It's a moggie". Duh!

I knitted him three sweaters in total, Mum never asked me who they were for. Each time one was finished I would take the train to London then the bus to Maidenhead and wait on the stairs to his flat until he came home. The fourth jumper I hadn't finished by the time we broke up, so I finished it off eventually and gave it to my husband; somehow I knitted one sleeve longer than the other which caused a lot of mirth and unpicking!

My father decided to build an extension on the back of our house so I offered to go and stay with Helen's parents for the duration, with an ulterior motive of course! More time with David when he came down. Linda was David and Helen's step-mother as their father was a widower. They had worked in the same office and when they retired they decided to get married and live by the sea in Seaford.

They were a lovely couple and churchgoers so they agreed I could stay there for a nominal rent as it was within walking distance to my job.

I waited impatiently for the weekend when David would drive down. He slept in the caravan in their garden and I had Helen's room as she was away. On my afternoon off from the surgery I went to Brighton by bus clothes shopping with my mother, as we often did. After getting off the bus at Pool Valley we'd walk through The Lanes to Western Road where the big stores were. We often bought the same outfits but in different colours. On this occasion I treated myself to a pale lemon, double layer, short and frilly, nylon nightdress, all the rage at the time and very feminine. I never told her, but I had a certain reason in my mind. After shopping and wandering back through The Lanes, we always went in the Lyons tea-rooms by the Old Steine for tea and cake served by a nippy waitress before we caught the bus home. Mum used to fall asleep on the bus missing all the lovely coastal views but I loved that ride, and still do.

David duly arrived and was surprised to find me staying there. We all ate dinner together then sat by the fire and read. His parents went to bed. Then he said we must turn in too and I should keep my window open. Lying in bed in my new nighty I watched the window and waited. Sure enough, a head popped in and it was him. He beckoned me to the window, helped me through it and led me by the hand to the caravan in the garden, creeping past his parent's bedroom window with our heads ducked down. It was a balmy summer night, we left the door open and cuddled up on the single divan. My nighty ended up around my neck, got in the way with all its frills so had to come off. Then his white Y fronts were tossed aside and then...well you know! This was it, this was what 'it' was supposed to be like, I was sure. Eventually I fell asleep and had the indignity of climbing back through the bedroom window in daylight but couldn't get back into bed as I had to get ready for work. We met at the breakfast table as if nothing had happened, except our eyes said it all.

When his parents went to church on Sundays, he would drive them there saying he was going to the other church, then drive back home where I was waiting and we would get it on in the hallway. We knew we had plenty of time so he undressed me slowly and lovingly then we lay together in my single bed. Too soon, he had to go and drive off back to Berkshire before his parents came back. I would lean out of the window with no clothes on to wave him off until next time. I was so in love it hurt.

Then there was a certain red telephone box in a twitten leading to Cricketfield Road; a useful place to 'shelter' when on the way to and from my bus stop after I had had to move back home. There was a special cove on the beach with the tide swishing around us. There was the back seat of his roomy car with the leather upholstery. Also the ruins and grass of Tide Mills. There was Mount Caburn with sheep for spectators.

After the extension was completed, however, I had to move back home again so our dates had to be kept secret from my parents who may or may not have known David came down weekends and holidays.

We had to have clandestine meetings but they were all the more romantic because of that. I thought so, anyway, especially when he did such things as write on the dusty bus window when he was waving me off after he met me from work and walked me to the bus stop. I had to go home from work, have dinner, wipe up the dishes, get changed, then I could bus back to Seaford where he would be waiting. What a performance!

I should have smelled a rat though, as he said we could not be seen out in public together while his divorce was decree nisi and not absolute. I didn't know anything about that sort of thing, I only knew how I felt. Like in the film *Truly, Madly, Deeply*. I was attracted to his lovely brown eyes, soft fair hair, engaging smile and sense of fun. We went to the cinema in Brighton sometimes with his sister in tow. I slipped my shoes off once and he teased me by hiding one, he got the usherette with her torch to help us look for it and then he eventually produced it with a big grin.

When Helen married John it was in Surrey where they came from. Another friend Carole and I went up by train. I had bought a new white furry hat with a black velvet band for the occasion, which I later wore to my own wedding and after that my toddler girls played with it and ruined it. It was a lovely big white church wedding. The bride walked up the aisle on her father's arm to the Trumpet Voluntary. We sat at the back on the bride's side and I was more interested in looking at the back of David's head than the bride and groom being married. The reception was at their aunt's house in Hazelmere. My present to the bride and groom was a large framed print called 'The Song of the Surf' which had cost me a weeks' wages in Eastbourne. But I thought it worth every penny.

In due course it was time for Carole and I to catch the train home. First David offered to drive us to the station, on the way there he offered to drive us down to Brighton, from where we could catch our local buses. We sat in the back of the car chatting about the wedding after taking off our fancy hats and I kept meeting his eyes in the mirror.

I did ask him to marry me once but he turned me down. I used to enjoy helping him mark his pupil's homework in his flat when I visited as he couldn't spell for toffee. He wrote the following at the top of one of his letters to me, which stays imprinted in my head:

*"Tis better to have loved and lost
than never to have loved at all"*

At Brighton bus station in he said to me, "Wait there" then he let Carole out of the car and we waved her goodbye.

As he opened the car door for me to get out, much to my surprise he said, "Come in the front and we'll go for a drive."

"I can't." I replied, "I have to be home for seven o'clock to look after my brothers."

That was the arrangement, every Saturday night I child minded while my dad took my mum out for a meal and a drink. But I couldn't resist the temptation, so we parked the car on the seafront by Palace Pier, went across the road to the hotel and asked permission to use the telephone in the foyer. I lied through my teeth that I was still at Helen's reception and would be home late.

But I guess my parents weren't daft because they got wise and my secret was out. I had been seeing David behind their backs. How I wish that I had stood up for myself. Dad was waiting to pounce when I finally got home, livid that they had missed their Saturday night out and yes, it was a shame for my mum, all dressed up and nowhere to go.

He shouted at me, "Where have you been? What time do you call this?" And worse, "The only thing he wants is what's between your legs." An embarrassingly true analysis!

Dad was red with rage and shaking with anger but he never raised his hand to me, he clenched his fists instead. He obviously thought I was still a virgin. My brother told me years later that they had their ears to the bedroom floor and could hear every word. Dad never gave me a front door key either; was that because you didn't become an adult until you were twenty-one back then, or was it because he didn't trust me? Both, I suspect!

Eventually the problem sorted itself out because David dumped me for another teacher, also named Helen. She used to write to his parents saying how much she loved him (I secretly read her letters when I was staying there). He married her I found out later. She was older and much more worldly-wise than I was, plus I never was any good at womanly wiles and I just wasn't mature enough to know how to hold onto him; the song *Take These Chains From My Heart* says it all and still makes me feel sad whenever I hear Ray Charles sing it. It took me ten years to get over him; they say you never forget your first love.

CHAPTER SEVEN

My life gets worse, as that episode with David led me into even more teenage trouble; my heart seemed to rule my head in those days. I'm not sure where sensible Virginia disappeared to, as it seemed to be the case of onwards and even more downwards with my next relationship.

One day at work a bloke came in with a bleeding head escorted by a chap asking if his workmate could be fitted in to see a doctor.

"Of course," I said, seeing the state he was in, so in no time at all he was patched up and off they went. My good deed for the day. The next day the chap came back to thank me. I told him that was what I was there for. He then asked me what time I finished work and could he meet me. He was tall and tanned with twinkling blue eyes, curly brown hair with sideburns, and looked and sounded nice so I said yes. He drove me home, past Tide Mills where I used to dally with David.

The second time Frank drove me home past Tide Mills he asked if I'd like to turn in there for a while.

I said, "No, thank you. I'd rather go straight home."

"Okay," he replied, "but tell me if you change your mind."

After only twenty-four hours thinking about it, I did change my mind so as we were heading towards Tide Mills on the third evening after work I said we could stop for a smoke so we drove in and parked up. The smoke turned into a snog and the back of his van turned out to be private and comfortable. Oh dear! The thing is, he really cared for me, he was really kind and nice and charming. I was not in love with him, although I was flattered by his attention and it felt good to be wanted again. So we had a fling.

Our flinging was mostly done in Angie and Bob's caravan; they were only too happy to go out to the pub leaving us to babysit for a few hours. He was older than me, had been in the war and had the scars to prove it. He was ashamed of these scars but to me his body and long legs were lovely, he was a fit and virile mature man.

It was far more than just that though. Frank met me from work regularly and as we were hitting it off we went on a lot of dates. We went to the pictures quite often, it was nice to sit down after a day's work, especially as I had to go home first to eat with the family and wait to dry the dishes. Then I'd change into the black polo neck sweater he had bought me, leaving my bra in my bedroom, as much for comfort as anything else (she lied), long before Women's Lib: and the burn your bra days. Finally, I ran back down the hill where he was still waiting, after dropping me off an hour or so before.

He took me to the wrestling matches in Brighton which was fun. I used to jump up and down shouting at the referee much to Frank's amusement. Once, on the way there we ran out of petrol, so he pushed the van into the side of the road in Saltdean and we jumped on a bus into Brighton to get some petrol with his spare but empty can. Sitting on the top deck he said words to the effect that his wife wouldn't have come on the bus with him, she would have stayed in the van complaining and sulking.

Pardon? What? Wife? Oh no, this can't be happening to me again, can it?

Then I thought about it and because I liked him, we got on well and I liked being taken out, I sort of ignored that problem because I wasn't married, so that was alright, wasn't it? We got the petrol and flagged down a lift back with a passing motorist; by now was too late for the wrestling that night so we drove up to Devil's Dyke.

We had lots of enjoyable times, more drives around the countryside with plenty of walks together because his building site was down by Seaford Head golf course as was his lodgings. He went home to his family in London most weekends. Sometimes we stayed in his workmate Rob's caravan on the building site playing cards or went for a drink in their boss's house with Rob's wife Angie and their baby. The boss's dog took a fancy to me one evening which the men thought was hilarious but I had the last laugh when we were wandering back across the site to the caravan, chatting. Getting no reply I turned round but Frank had disappeared. Down a great big hole in the ground. So I just stood there convulsed with laughter watching him trying to clamber out. He finally managed it after several attempts. That's what too much alcohol does!

I had come to know Angie as a patient at the surgery, she used to telephone in the evenings when I was on duty and I listened whilst ushering the patients in and out. She rang from the site office so it didn't cost her anything but she was suffering from post-natal depression, was far from home and needed to talk to someone. That too was my job. We became good friends, the four of us, and I was eighteen by now so could officially go into pubs for a drink, but only if escorted by a man, as was the custom of the day.

Our favourite pub was The Star in Alfriston; those were my gin and orange and rum and pep days. It is said that Sussex men only have one drink when they go to the pub but my friends weren't from Sussex! I was however, but my mindset was:

"Sussex wunt be druv"

Whenever Susan Maughan's *Bobby's Girl* was played on the van's radio Frank would sing along with it changing Bobby's Girl to Ginny's Boy and I remember the smile on his face and the look in his eyes as he sang it to me.

# # # # # # #

I got a bit squiffy one night so after I had said goodnight and checked my watch I decided to climb in through my bedroom window, instead of ringing the doorbell and getting my dad out of bed to let me in. There was a double extension ladder in our back garden so I extended it, put it up against my window and climbed all the way up. Only to find my mum had closed the window. It was shut tight.

I could not get in.

So back down the ladder in my high heels I went, closed the ladder down, put it back where I got it from, sighed, and tottered round to the front door to ring the bell.

Ding dong ding dong, rang the musical chime, it wasn't the first time I'd had to do that either.

Dad let me in without a word and off I crept, shoes now in hand, to my bedroom. The next morning I realised I had extended the time of my home-coming because of the ladder incident and I must have been drunk. I could have broken my neck too. But hey! I was never late for work, so that was okay, wasn't it?

Another night I missed the last bus home (again) and rang him from a Seaford phone box to come and fetch me. He told me to go inside the train station's waiting room and wait. It seemed such a long wait until he walked in and then I noticed he only had his jacket on over his pyjamas. I was sure I was in double trouble that time. But nothing was said and it was a long silent drive home.

I'm so sorry Daddy, I must have driven you nuts at times.

I think that was the final straw for my long-suffering dad, he was fed up with coming out looking for me, picking me up when I had missed the last bus home, or letting me in late on a work night, so he decided he couldn't handle me anymore and threatened to make me a Ward of the Court if I didn't behave myself. I have no idea what that would have meant for me as I was still under age. However, as I didn't think I was doing anything wrong I carried on with my social life as normal. And was never late for work - except once, when I had overslept in the caravan and Miss Allenby had phoned home to ask if I was ill only to be told I wasn't there because it was my night to sleep-over on duty at the lady doctor's house. Which was my cover story. I really did sleep there for extra pay sometimes when it was her turn on night duty. She had geese as guard dogs and introduced me to yoghurt and German evening classes.

"Guten Abend"

Dad must have had a re-think and talked to Mum and Gran about what to do about me because the next thing I knew he told me that we needed a break from each other so he was sending me away. Splitting us up, that's what he was doing. I could choose between Cheshire and Devon, where we had relatives. I had been to Cheshire with Gran before to visit her sister but had never been to Devon so I opted for the latter. I have never owned up before but I had already given in my notice at work and had been applying for other jobs. So even I did not know what I was doing or wanted to do. I have the same outlook today. Looking back, I suspect that miserable middle-aged spinster Miss Allenby must have kept my parents informed. One of the firms I had a job offer from was as a secretary in an aircraft factory in Hertfordshire, where Angie came from and where they were going back to when their work contract came to an end.

Sometime before this and after David ditched me I had already applied to be a policewoman but was turned down because I wore glasses. I'd also applied to emigrate to Australia on a £10 assisted passage by ship, which would have taken six weeks to get there. I fancied that. I had corresponded with my godmother aunt in Melbourne who said they would vouch for me and I could stay on their sheep farm until I got a secretarial job in Melbourne. Super! Then my dad said I had to wait until I was twenty-one. But a lot more happened before then.

I guess my intention before the Devon decision was to go with Angie and Bob to her mother's house in Hatfield and take up that job offer. My parents found out about that because they intercepted my post, they used to open it or hide it and all I got was the flack. Dad had other ideas because he was still responsible for me. My aunt and uncle, not blood relations but close friends of my parents, used to run The

Spanish Lady pub in Saltdean and had relocated to The Masons Arms pub in Torquay. I don't remember whether my train ticket was a single or return but I do remember sitting on that train. I think the plan was I should stay with them for three weeks and then go back home after the enforced break.

The following Monday morning in the not so merry month of May, I said goodbye to my mum who had her cleaning lady in and was busying herself with housework as usual. My dad had already gone to work and my brothers had gone to school. I cannot remember whether I said goodbye to them or not. Probably not. I went downstairs, leaving most of my personal possessions and clothes behind in my little bedroom, taking one last look through the kitchen window down the garden to Tess our Alsatian dog, who was such a good friend and companion to me; we shared some wonderful times together, as we'd had her since she was a puppy.

But today I was on my own. I walked through the garage with only my handbag and suitcase. I carried it down the Drove where I used to walk to school, and I boarded the steam train to Torquay. The world was my oyster, I was a free agent, or so I thought. But fate intervened and I never did take that particular return journey home. Eighteen months would pass before I returned for a short visit.

CHAPTER EIGHT

During August 1943 in London two sisters were heavily pregnant. They had married their soldier sweethearts the previous year in a double registry office wedding but as their husbands were away in the war fighting the Jerries, they were living with their parents. Dorothy went into labour first followed six days later by Florence. After the obligatory ten days in the Maternity ward they were each allowed home with their new bundles of joy.

Their father was a butcher by day, in the evenings he read the newspaper and smoked his pipe but when the air raid sirens sounded he bundled his wife, daughters and granddaughters into the cupboard under the stairs while he stood outside the front door scanning the sky.

Florence's husband came home on leave and it would be nice to say that he advised his wife with their new baby to evacuate to a Sussex village, to live with his mother in safety, but the truth of the matter was their own mother just couldn't cope with two daughters and two baby granddaughters, so after three weeks of living in the same house, my cousin and I were split up to live separate lives.

Kristina and her mum continued to live with her parents because when Bill came home from the war, Dorothy decided she didn't love him anymore and wanted a divorce. Meanwhile, we were ensconced in my gran's Rodmell cottage, where we all got along fine. Every September Mum took us to stay with her parents for a week, and every Easter Gran and Granddad came to stay with us.

While staying in London I remember sitting on the stairs playing buses with Kris. I always had to be the passenger sitting halfway up the stairs while she was the driver sitting on the bottom stair. She was also the conductor. I had to stand at the bottom of the stairs after Kris had set herself up, she would allow me onto the 'bus' then follow me up the stairs to my chosen seat saying, "Tickets please" and giving me a carefully prepared piece of paper in exchange for a halfpenny. She followed the routine of the old London buses, stopping and starting at many bus stops, letting her passengers (me) on and off saying, "Hold tight" ringing her conductor's bell borrowed from the dining room and driving the bus to the next stop.

We played pretend tea-parties in the back garden, down by the blackberry bushes, squashing ripe berries onto pieces of bread for our cakes and using water from the garden tap for our tea. We played dressing-up using our mums' and grans' clothes, shoes, hats and bags; nothing was bought from the shops because of the war and the rationing during and afterwards.

We went to Granddad's shop together to collect the meat for dinner and a regular outing was to nearby Broomfield Park, which was a large area with lots of things to do including a lake to sail boats, a swing park, tennis courts, lawns to sit and make daisy chains on, a bandstand with a brass band playing on Sundays and lots of deckchairs. Dorothy met her second husband during this time and he became a doting dad to Kristina because he couldn't have children of his own. He and Dorothy were married when Kris was five and when she was older they changed her surname to his by deed poll.

During my school summer holidays I was put on the coach to Ramsgate to spend two weeks with them. They had bought a new bungalow and Granny and Grandad had also bought a house there. Kris used to freely come and go between her parents' house and our grandparents' house, having her own bedroom in both places, so our maternal Granny clearly loved her like my paternal Gran loved me. Kris only had one Gran but I had two.

We were happy-go-lucky girls on our holidays together in Ramsgate. She used to take me to

Dreamland, a big fun arcade down by the harbour. We would cycle to Pegwell Bay where the Viking ship is, walk to the beach and the local riding stables or bus to the cinema, depending on the weather.

In the cinema queue she would say, "Follow me" and proceed to chat up a pair of likely looking boys. Somehow she got them to pay for our admission. We would all sit together, then just before the end of the film she would tell them we had to go to the Ladies. They nodded happily, fully expecting us to return. Crafty Kristina had other ideas and we legged it out of the exit door running down to Dreamland to spend the money we had saved. She was always the leader and I was her follower, just like on the bus on the stairs.

Kris was also well in with the riding stables and took me there to help muck out, for which she got a free ride on Sixpence, a big black horse, while I just watched and waited. One night in the bed we shared top to toe (she used to tickle my hand while I tickled her feet), she whispered, "Get dressed" and then from under the bed pulled out a torch and some food. With a finger on her lips she led me to the lounge window. We climbed through it, put on the welly boots she had left under it and off we went by torchlight back to the stables to play strip poker with some boys whom I had never met before. (We were all young so nobody stripped off completely, it was just a bit of innocent fun). After our midnight feast and card games, we went back home in the pitch black in the middle of the night, back through the window and into bed. Kristina had no fear, but I was too scared and refused to go again.

She got engaged once, aged eighteen, to a boy named Alan. Her Mum and Dad liked him and welcomed him into their home. After a few months, they rented a flat and moved in together. Ten days later Kristina moved back in with her parents, calling off the engagement saying, "I'm not washing his socks." Honestly, she really did say that!

That is how Kris spent the rest of her life, never living with a man again. She had men friends and she had sugar daddies, and she always dated men with money.

In January of 1963, shortly before I moved to Devon, I was snowed off from work and her parents were away, so we stayed together in their bungalow in Newhaven near our house. Our grandparents had passed away by then and Dorothy and step-dad Rob had left Ramsgate to come and live near us. The sisters were together again. This was a shame for me because I had left school and Mum had started treating me like an adult, going out shopping and to the cinema together, alternating between Brighton and Eastbourne, until her sister came and spoiled it, leaving me left out. Staying with Kris that week was the best time for me, like having a real sister again and no brothers. We lounged about, watched the telly, did each other's make-up and hair, played records and smoked and drank a little.

Kris always walked round the house holding an ashtray but my ash keeps dropping on the floor and I have to get the vacuum cleaner out.

She worked all her life, firstly working and lodging in a riding stables in Kent, then she had several spells as an au pair in Texas, having become fond of travel and foreign holidays by now. She had her last sexual encounter aged thirty-five with a Spanish waiter, and told me some years later, she didn't like the mess involved. She said she had no idea how I could be married and have five children, she could not picture me like that. I don't think she ever saw us all together as a family. But we always kept in touch throughout our separate lives. Kris and I were close because our mothers were sisters who only had one daughter each.

When I was expecting my second baby she came to stay in our flat supposedly to help me, but the only thing she liked doing was going shopping. She was fastidious and elegant in smart or casual clothes, with long glossy dark brown hair and brown eyes. Even when her hair turned grey she kept it long, tied back in a ponytail and drifted around in long skirts which seemed to suit her laid-back lifestyle.

We were sitting on the sofa sewing one evening in 1965 when my husband came home from the pub so Kris jumped up and disappeared into her bedroom while I went into the kitchenette to fetch his dinner. He sat down on the sofa, right on top of the needle Kris had left stuck in it. I never heard the last of that, he swore she did it on purpose, and knowing Kris, she probably did! He hammered on her bedroom door shouting at her so the next day she went home and that was the end of my home-help. When I mentioned it on the phone years later, Kris just laughed and carried on slurping her wine!

She has two dachshunds named Coogie Bear and Trousers and several cats during her lifetime. Her favourite cat was Bubbles, Bubbs for short, she'd feed him from her plate with her fingers. She also used to go down in the lift to feed the stray cats every evening in the bin area of the flats and planned to leave her estate to animal charities.

In her later working life Kris worked for Marks and Spencer in Brighton for nineteen years, retiring with a nice pension. She stocked up the frozen food cabinets which made her hands bad, sometimes they had to be treated with cortisone cream and bandaged up so she was off work. The cabinets were deep and cold she said, so it could have been frostbite, even with the special gloves on.

She was living back with her parents again, never having rented or bought her own home. Her dad died first and then her mum which left Kris in the Brighton flat by herself, eleven floors up with two bedrooms and a balcony. I stayed there several times. We had fun going food shopping - Brighton has a large gay population so we acted up to that and nobody batted an eyelid! Kris got bored with Brighton and the British weather after retirement and decided to move to Denia in Spain where she sadly passed away aged seventy-one. She liked her evening drink and cigarettes. I will miss her husky voice and her attitude and regret I never had the chance to go to Spain to visit her.

Her friends scattered her ashes on Montgo mountain near Denia, a Spanish wildlife reserve, because she didn't want any fuss.

CHAPTER NINE

The train chugged its way along the track to London Victoria via Lewes and Brighton, all familiar territory to me gazing out of the carriage window. Next I had to cross London from Victoria to Paddington, so not fancying negotiating the Tube trains and because I had a long journey ahead of me, I hailed a black cab. These taxis were like beetles scurrying around London all day and all night. The same with the big red double-decker buses; if you just missed one another one would loom into view immediately.

The hour it took to arrive in London passed quickly. I'd done this trip several times before; once to apply for an emigration form at Australia House, another time to go to an interview for the television game show 'Double Your Money' with spelling as my chosen subject - in a posh hotel with a red six inch thick carpet, or so it felt when my heels sank in, and several other times to go sight-seeing or window-shopping along Oxford Street.

Safely on the brown and cream liveried Westcountry train I put my suitcase in the net rack above the seats and filled with anticipation I settled into a corner seat on the window side, not on the corridor side of the carriage. It would be a six hour journey to an unknown destination and little did I know then that my life was at a cross-roads. I just thought I was taking an early summer holiday between jobs and away from the animosity at home. A seaside break would be good and I felt happy and free.

I had forgotten to pack a book to read on the journey, which by now had changed to unending countryside, having passed by all the interesting backyards, so I decided to write a "Dear John" letter to Frank because I already knew that his contract in Seaford was coming to an end but he did not know I was going away, so this time I could finish with him in a nice explanatory letter before he finished with me like David had. He was a nice guy but I was not in love with him like I had been with David; I think he was a substitute. Besides, as well as a wife he had children.

After composing my flowery letter I was still in a pensive mood so instead of gazing at the passing landscape with negative thoughts and with nothing to read except the holiday posters on the wall of the carriage, I wrote a fairy story which revolved around a Fairy Mairy who fluttered all over London looking for her kin. It was an odd contrast; a bright winged pixie flying not over green hills and dales but blocks of flats and terraced houses which were grey with grime from the smog filled air. Nevertheless Fairy Mairy visited all the landmarks I knew in London which I considered to be the best city in the whole wide world, a bustling metropolis with people scurrying about their business like ants and a far cry from the Sussex landscape which I knew so well. I suppose the story was a projection of how I felt; young and naively optimistic about life even though I'd been effectively exiled – cut off from my own life in Sussex and left to drift the streets of London for a while looking for the kin I had left behind.

########

My train chugged into Torquay station around six pm and stopped with a big sigh of steam, which is exactly how I felt. I got off and hailed a taxi to the address my dad had given me. It was a pub in Babbacombe not far from where I live now. Torquay station is just off the sea front so the taxi ride took me along the coast road; this was my first glimpse of the English Riviera. Here the sea is blue, in Sussex it is more green than blue due to all the chalk.

In hindsight I think my dad made a daft decision sending me to a pub, especially as he didn't trust men. The reason for that lack of trust was because he got all the blame when his teenage sister was impregnated by her Canadian soldier during the war, even though he was away in the Army at the time; as my mum explained to me many years later.

I was nineteen and NOT a barmaid, but the locals assumed I was because 'uncle' John had asked me to come down into the bar from their flat in the evening to attract the younger punters, the crafty bugger! Sheila and John had no children of their own, goodness knows what my dad had said about me on the phone, but they had known me since I was twelve. Sheila was lovely, a small bubbly blonde, but she wasn't young. We went shopping together afternoons when the pub was closed. It was refurbished while I stayed there, but when I arrived it was a spit and sawdust place frequented by old men. I could see John's point of view, and anyway I was under his roof and care.

On my second evening there Sheila and I had gone upstairs leaving John to close up. We heard a din going on so when he came upstairs Sheila asked him what it was about to which he replied, "Just a couple of drunks who didn't want to leave so they had to be ejected." On the third evening when I went downstairs those two 'drunks' were sitting in the window seat. The good looking one came up to the bar and asked me for a pint of bitter. I said truthfully I did not know how to pull pints. He laughingly replied that didn't matter, just give it a go. So I did and he got a glassful of froth with not much beer. He told me to wait for the froth to settle and top it up, then duly paid for it with 'one for yourself' and went back to his seat, smiling at me all the time. I served myself a Babycham, lit a cigarette, put a record on the Jukebox and hovered about like John wanted. I had only been there two days when this chancer asked me if I would like to take the pub's dogs for a walk at closing time. Yes, I would and yes, I did. His name was Chris.

It's about half a mile from the back of the pub's beer garden across Wall's Hill to the cricket pavilion. The dogs loved it running free as at 11pm there was no-one else about. The pavilion had a veranda and as soon as we got there Chris took off his duffle coat and spread it out on said veranda. Then he invited me to sit down on it. He sat down beside me. Pretty soon we were snogging and one thing led to another...which didn't take long. What is it with men? My dad was right, they only wanted one thing, young or old, they're all the same.

We walked the dogs back to the pub and were kissing by the ice-cream parlour on the corner when along came John with his torch looking for me. He told Chris off and told him to clear off, told me to get indoors as he was responsible for me and said he was going to telephone my father - who had sent me there to avoid these situations in the first place. Sigh.

That was my introduction to my future husband.

There is an interesting monochrome film that was made in this area in 1964, it is called The System, directed by Michael Winner and starring Oliver Reed. It accurately depicts what happens to girls on their summer holidays in Torquay, the English seaside resort, during the early 1960's. Which means I was just one of many! I never knew about the film until recently, now I have it on DVD.

From the day Chris first set eyes on me until the day he died, he never looked at another woman, although they looked at him when we were out and about, mostly pub crawling that first summer. His other love was alcohol so I was flattered but often felt second best; this heart rules the head thing was a pain in the bum.

He was normal height but when I wore my stiletto winkle-picker shoes I was taller than him so I used to walk in the gutter - I had no problem with his image, only with my own. He had a stocky build, swarthy complexion and hands like shovels. His jet black hair was greased and combed into a DA (duck's arse) style just like Elvis Presley but Elvis was on another continent whereas this one was only in another county and I found him - or rather he found me! When he ran out of Brylcreem he used margarine which made the seagulls land on his head down the harbour and on Oddicombe beach where he had spent a lot of his youth; his dad being the seasonal speedboat driver for a trip round the bay. His dark brown eyes showed every emotion and he came from the Romany gypsies on his mum's side. He wore a scruffy black duffle coat and had gregarious ways; definitely not a wimp in a suit. All this I found irresistibly attractive. So that was it, my fate was sealed. I tried to find out things about him but he wasn't very forthcoming. "Where do you live?" "Over the hill" he replied, pointing up the road. His mate told me they were both single so that was a relief. He wasn't a thinker or a talker, he was a doer. The strong silent type but honest and genuine if a bit erm, forceful. And different. Life was never dull with Chris.

I had fallen head over heels in love again and couldn't bear to be apart, although we only met evenings initially. He seemed to reciprocate my feelings but then I found out there was more to it than that. He was twenty-one and self-employed, earning good money scrapping metal, (later also becoming a tree surgeon - in great demand because he was not afraid of heights or climbing dangerous trees). Sometimes he earned as much in one morning as an office worker earned in a week. But he was homeless when we met having been locked out of his parents house for the umpteenth time due to his temper. That was something we had in common - not a temper but issues with our parents. On the whole I think it was a case of opposites attract, with mutual needs.

He made no secret of the fact he was looking for a wife, he told me so, having been advised to settle down by his concerned sister and witnessing his brother's family life when he visited them. He even went as far as asking a fortune-teller gypsy friend Betty to read my palm and tell me I would marry him. She waylaid me in the hallway of Sheila's pub one evening when I was on my way to the theatre to see Adam Faith. I crossed her palm with silver and shrugged it off at the time but had often wondered since whether it really was in my lifeline to read - and then only last year when we asked him again, he smiled and half-admitted that he had put Betty up to it. That burst my bubble as I had thought it was fate.

After we met we had dinner out every evening; steak and chips, fish and chips, Chinese (a first for him but my favourite), a dessert for me and the bill for him.

I was very happy with my holiday romance so I thought about staying on in Torquay for the summer, find a job as an hotel receptionist, leave Sheila and John's home and rent a bedsit. John phoned Dad about my plans, especially about my seeing Chris on Wall's Hill after closing time, so my parents drove down the next weekend to try to persuade me to return home with them. Tears all round but I refused because I was still hurting from being sent away and I was enjoying my new found freedom away from my dad. Chris and I slept out under the stars before I found us somewhere to live, once on Petitor Downs with newspapers for mattresses on the bench seat in the shelter - I awoke next morning to find him chasing a pheasant but he didn't catch it - and one night on Wall's Hill it started raining so we ran from our sea view bench and slept under a rather prickly hedge. Another time, being too drunk to walk and too skint for a cab, we stopped halfway back to our caravan and bedded down for the night in a farmer's barn. Chris was snoring with his coat over his head when I saw a flashing light bobbing towards me. It was the local copper with a torch. He questioned me then advised me to go back home to Sussex. I meekly said, "Yes, sir" but didn't of course. Chris cut loose the farmer's largest marrow on leaving the next morning and we took it to his sister's house to exchange it for a bath and breakfast.

After our family talk in Sheila's flat I went back to the pub along the road where Dad had found me sitting with Chris, his dad and brothers, to find Chris sitting alone in the beer garden. His face lit up when he saw me walk in, he said he thought he would never see me again. But there I was, with my mind made up to stay in Torquay for the rest of the summer. My parents drove down again after I had written to tell them I was pregnant. This time I wanted to go back home. I asked if I could go and live with my gran in Rodmell, but Dad said "No you will dishonour the family name I have built up."

That is another instance of his sister and her Canadian soldier messing with my dad's head and it rebounding on me. He said the next time I come here I want to see you two get married.

So the third time they came down was to witness our wedding in November on the Saturday before President Kennedy was assassinated. Dad then washed his hands of me and told Chris I was now his responsibility but asked me what I would like for a wedding present. That was easy, we had previously seen a red Bedford Dormobile van for sale down the road, just right for work and pleasure with nice high-up seats, sliding doors and plenty of room in the back all for £30. The two men went off and bought it straightaway. On the Monday we drove it to Plymouth to take it for a spin and buy me a wedding ring as I only had the 7/6d marriage certificate. This trip was eventful, first the van boiled up, then we drove the wrong way up a one way street and got honked at a lot before realising, then my swollen finger (a symptom of pregnancy) was too large for the rings we could afford so I ran out of the shop in tears. The jeweller and Chris chased me down the street and coaxed me back into the shop where the nice man gave me a more expensive 22 carat gold band for the fiver we could afford.

I had met and married Chris all within the space of six months and that was the happiest time of my life. In those days girls used to worry we would be left on the shelf - an old maid, a spinster - if we weren't married by the time we were twenty-one so there was a lot of pressure on us. After we were married I was expected to look after the children and be a housewife, not have a job and go out to work, because he said he would look after me. I only kept in touch with my best school friend Brenda as I was actively discouraged to keep in touch with anybody else from Sussex, except my relatives.

I didn't go back 'home' for eighteen months. When the baby was six months old we drove there to show her off to my parents and family for the first time. We took my brother back, he had been sent down by coach to stay with us during his summer holidays. When we arrived Tessa bounded up the garden path wagging her tail; when she met me in the doorway, she put her paws on my shoulders and licked my face all over which brought tears to my eyes, a lump in my throat and a sick feeling in my stomach. Happy but homesick at the same time as well as a strong sense of déjà vu.

CHAPTER TEN

Here in Torbay on the English Riviera, the upmarket word for bedsits is flatlets. These are basically furnished one-room living, with the lounge, kitchen and bedroom all in one space, and the shared bathroom facilities out in a corridor somewhere, or even on another floor of the building.

Back in the early 1960s there didn't seem many health and safety rules, but I do recall an oblong red metal fire extinguisher in the communal entrance hall, because it's bracket fell off the wall one day and the extinguisher exploded shooting foam all over the place. We tenants just walked through it until somebody else cleaned it up!

The Landlords were an elderly couple from oop North who chose to retire to a large Victorian house down here by the sea. To afford this they had to rent out their first and second floor rooms keeping the ground floor living space for themselves. They were the ones who had to clean up the foam filled entrance hall. The drawback of my particular bedsit was the communal bathroom up a flight of dodgy stairs into the attic room under the eaves. Everyone had to put a shilling (five pence) into the electricity meter to get hot water for a bath. There was another money-grabbing meter in my room as well, in case I wanted the light on, or heaven forbid, use the electric fire! I had to eat out mainly because the cooking facilities were less than minimal, but I was lucky that my job on the reception desk at the Links Hotel in St. Marychurch enabled me to have my dinner there, and the hotel was close enough to be able to walk to work.

I received clean bedding once a week included in the rent cost. One day the landlady knocked on the door with the clean bedding in her arms and said, "I'm glad I found you in, I want a word with you. We caught your boyfriend climbing out of the window this morning and had been wondering why your sheets were so dirty."

Oh heck! No answer to that!

She continued, "We have decided to give you one week's notice to vacate the flatlet" - and off she marched. Mrs Stenhouse was her name, forever after called Mother Henhouse by me. Chris came home from work (through the window as usual) and I made him sleep in the armchair because the communal bathroom facilities were upstairs and I didn't want him to be spotted again.

My job lasted about as long as that bedsit. I got instant dismissal after only three weeks due to undercharging a customer when he asked for his bill on leaving. The other receptionist hadn't prepared his bill even though I had asked her to, spiteful cow, so I did the sums, presented the bill, he paid up and went on his merry way with his two sons. One satisfied customer, I thought. But when the Manager checked it later, my mistake was discovered and I was told not to return at the end of my shift. I was given my wages plus a week in advance and off I went, head hung in shame, to meet Chris in the pub. On the way, I passed a shoe shop so to console myself I popped in and bought not one but two pairs of high heeled shoes, one in black and the other in red. Neither Chris nor my parents nagged me about losing my first job here, in fact they were all very good about it, but I didn't feel very good about it. Especially as the next job I applied for was as a seasonal waitress in a small greasy spoon type cafe; I saw the ad. and walked in to apply but wasn't taken on as I'd had no relevant experience!

The day after being told off by Mother Henhouse I telephoned a taxi on my way home from work and crept off into the night - into a local caravan park actually - that I had also telephoned from work. I hired a grotty little caravan as a couple in Maidencombe, on the edge of Torquay, which meant we now had to catch a bus to work every day and we pinched a pint of milk to drink off the doorstep opposite the bus stop while waiting. We rolled home one night to find a padlock nearly as big as the door locking us out. So we camped out in a nearby garage until our landlord drove by on his motorbike. Then we went and faced him - rather, Chris did while I hid behind him. An argument ensued but on payment of last weeks' rent he said he would unlock the door, so we scrabbled about in our pockets and purse and found enough money. But first we had to go into his large fancy caravan and sign a contract over a stamp, begrudgingly I might add, but it was late by then and raining so it was the only thing we could do.

I practised my cooking skills in that caravan, the Baby Belling cooker was in the middle of it, the double bed with itchy old Army blankets and no sheets, filled one end by the door, and the seating area with a table in the middle was down the window end with views over the countryside - to where our eldest daughter lives now so these days I can look across from her house when I go outside for a smoke, see where we were living and reminisce. There was a small shop on site and a communal washing line. Nowadays the caravans are long gone and private houses line the lane while cows graze in the field. We had no television (the only thing I did miss from home), but we had a radio that I had been given from home and still have now, and in the evenings after work we frequented local pubs. Sussex people only have one drink when they go to the pub, if you remember, but Devonshire dumplings, well, let's just say there were an abundance of cider apple orchards around back then and if you drank enough Scrumpy you could make music with two spoons or a penny and a halfpenny, while singing the Wurzels' *The Blackbird Song*. Even walk like an Egyptian which Chris's brother was good at. Chris could put away four pints an hour while I had the one drink and did the crossword puzzle in the newspaper.

The caravan was jacked up onto grass with no hard standings there, so when I carried our plates of home-made dinner to the table after it had rained, the caravan would tip forward as the legs sunk into the soft grass. Often our dinners went all over the table especially when I had made gravy, as I tipped forwards too. I had to persevere though because there were no supermarket ready meals in those days, not even supermarkets, just individual shops selling their own goods; the butcher, the baker (but no candlestick maker), the grocer and the greengrocer, etcetera. I also cooked because the way to a man's heart is through his stomach, so I was told!

Talking of stomachs, mine began to swell. Oh dear, now I was in the soup, erm no, in the family way actually and I could see my new found independence flying out of the window together with my dreams. I saw a spinster lady doctor and she confirmed it. Then she said, "I presume you are going to marry the father?" and that was the only option I was given. During this pregnancy I changed from a girl into a woman; my body changed and so did my mindset. The sex, drugs and rock n roll lifestyle was out. Time for a new chapter now.

I wrote to my mother. My parents drove down from Sussex soon after, discussions were held, plans were made, and it all culminated in a shotgun wedding in the registry office at Newton Abbot, which I paid for, not my father as was supposed to be the tradition. I was now exiled in Devon forever, goodbye to Sussex.

I want to add here that we were married and stayed faithful to each other for over fifty-one years, until the day he passed away suddenly and silently here at home, with me holding his hand. This is why I am now writing this book for our children and grandchildren.

Our wedding was a simple affair, we wore our best clothes and I wore the hat I had bought for Helen's wedding. Chris went to his parents house that morning while I got ready, then my parents with my two younger brothers still in short trousers came to pick me up. Mum said I could sit in the front seat of the car. Chris's dad and one brother came but not his mum, I have no idea why she didn't as I never asked her but Chris was her favourite son and gave her money so I think she wasn't too happy about sharing him.

The only advice she ever gave me was, if your minced meat has gone off, add vinegar and they'll never know!

We didn't invite or even tell anybody else. Our dads were our witnesses. Chris said, "My awful wedded wife" instead of lawful wedded wife which I constantly teased him about; it probably rang true at times anyway.

After handing me over, my father said he was hungry, so we drove to the Drive Inn at Buckland where some of us had dinner, and one bottle of champagne which Dad paid for. 'Some of us' means he wouldn't pay for Chris's Dad and brother to eat so Chris wouldn't eat with us either. I don't blame him! That was the extent of my wedding breakfast and reception. But it proves to me you don't need a fancy white frock, flowers, cake and all the trimmings to be properly married, and more importantly, to stay married. After that we went our separate ways, my parents, brothers and I; they drove back to sunny Sussex while I stayed down in Devon with my new husband.

CHAPTER ELEVEN

Virginia sat on the bank with her head in her hands and the stones in her pockets, mesmerised by the fast flowing river. She had left the church after her brothers' memorial service saying she was going for a walk and wanted to be alone. This was it, crunch time. Sink or swim. Her mind was in a whirl and her thoughts were random black invasions. Maybe the tears to release her from the pain of life would come if she sat here for a little while longer. If they didn't, she had already put the stones in her coat pockets and was ready to wade in and sink into oblivion. Virginia heard the church clock strike four and decided to wait until half past to see if the turmoil within her head would stop, or whether she would take the next and final step.

"Please God, make it stop" she cried out loud. Here and now her life was at a crossroads, would it be onwards and upwards or would it be onwards and downwards?

# # # # # # #

On April 19, 1941, THE ASSOCIATED PRESS reported the following:

Mrs. Woolf's Body Found
Verdict of Suicide Is Returned in Drowning of Novelist

LONDON, April 19 -- Dr. E. F. Hoare, Coroner at New Haven, Sussex, gave a verdict of suicide today in the drowning of Virginia Woolf, novelist who had been bombed from her home twice. Her body was recovered last night from the River Ouse near her week-end house at Lewes.

The Coroner read a note that Mrs. Woolf had left for her husband, Leonard.

"I have a feeling I shall go mad," the note read. "I cannot go on any longer in these terrible times. I hear voices and cannot concentrate on my work. I have fought against it but cannot fight any longer. I owe all my happiness to you but cannot go on and spoil your life."

Her husband testified that Mrs. Woolf had been depressed for a considerable length of time.

When their Bloomsbury home was wrecked by a bomb some time ago, Mr. and Mrs. Woolf moved to another nearby. It, too, was made uninhabitable by a bomb, and the Woolfs then moved to their weekend home in Sussex.

Mrs. Woolf, who was 59, vanished March 28.

However, that opening scene by the river Ouse which I have repeated from the beginning of this book does not refer to Virginia Woolf.

There were two Virginia's contemplating an end on that riverbank. The second Virginia was me. Twenty-five years after Virginia Woolf ended her life I had been driven to the brink of despair.

# # # # # # #

Eddy was the quiet one, the middle sibling of us three, and for the past fifty years my younger brother and I have had to live without him. I have often wondered what he would be doing, where he would be living, would he be married and how many children would they have had? He had a girlfriend, Sarah, when he had his accident. I always remember his birth date in December and the date he died in June.

I was married with a new baby and a toddler when I heard the news. We'd recently had to move flats again because the mean landlord and his wife could get more rent as summer lets, so our winter let time was up. He said we could go back after the holiday season, but you can imagine what we replied to that, and drove away with our babies and belongings on bad terms.

Because it was difficult to find a flat that would accept children all we could find to live in was another old caravan with no running water on a site down a steep hill, the other side of

Paignton. The toilet was in a shed in the middle of a field where everybody could see you queuing up and inside you could hear them complaining about waiting and asking each other who was in there! I utilised my baby's potty sometimes, until the day the postman knocked on the caravan door right next to me while I was otherwise engaged. I just held my breath until he went away, luckily the babies were sleeping so it appeared that no-one was home!

The next week I had to take the baby back to the clinic to be weighed again so while we were over that way, my husband left us in the car while he went into our old flats to ask if there was any post. He was gone for some time but I wasn't worried, thinking he was giving them another piece of his mind.

I can see my husband now, fifty years on, walking down the drive towards us in the car parked on the other side of the road. I looked at his face before he had even crossed the road and felt something, a premonition, expecting to be told some bad news, but not the bombshell he dropped on me when he got back in the car.

My brother was dead. Killed in a motorbike accident. Last week. Two hundred and fifty miles away. Back home in Sussex.

We drove along the road to the local shops where my husband got a pound's worth of change for the telephone box so I could phone home. Being a new mother myself I was wondering how my mum was feeling, what would she say and what could I say?

She didn't make much sense over the phone (my dad told me later that she had been medicated by the family doctor), but I managed to find out a few facts. A heart wrenching one was that my parents had telephoned the flats last week when the accident happened to tell me but we had moved out and not left a forwarding address or telephone number, because we had rowed with the landlord. So they had no way of contacting me. To this day I still dislike private landlords, money grabbing machines that they are!

All this time my father had not been very friendly towards me so I was glad that I had my husband for support and at least my father was there for my mother and other brother.

They lived on the Lewes road between Piddinghoe and Southease at the time, next to the old churchyard, in a new bungalow they'd had built after I left home. As we lived in Torquay, Dad said, "Don't come to the funeral because you have just had a baby, wait and come to the memorial service later on."

I could cope with that because just a few weeks previously, at Easter, my gran, Eddy and his motorbike had come to Devon by train to spend a few days with us before I had the baby because they missed me. They had stayed in a vacant flat, while we were still at the old flats before we'd had to leave. We drove to Exeter railway station to meet them and save them changing trains to get to Torquay. Gran rode in the van with us while Eddy rode alongside on his motorbike. We had a lovely weekend together before he had to go back home for work but my gran stayed on for the week; she would have stayed longer except my husband upset her. Eddy wanted me to ride pillion on his bike to the shops and back before he went home but I said no because I was heavily pregnant; ever since his accident I wish I had said yes. When I stood at the bottom of the drive and waved him off, that was the last time I ever saw him. I can still picture the scene now.

My mum's mother went to stay with her bereaved daughter and would you believe it, she fell and broke her leg while she was there, and she had to stay in my brother's bedroom which upset my mum even more because she wanted to leave it as Eddy had left it. It is a good thing there's medication because I cannot comprehend how a mother can cope with losing a child and I sincerely hope I never have to experience that.

I have still got the newspaper cuttings about the accident, the tributes and the enquiry, all faded and brown with age now, along with some things of Eddy's that my dad had kept out in his shed, and gave to me for safe-keeping when he knew he had terminal cancer. Eddy's school books and pens, his erasure and sheath knife from Switzerland in particular. My mother had kept her son's pyjamas. I found them in her drawer when I cleared out her house after she died. With only myself and my brother left now and no male heir to carry on our name, the Sussex Dedman's are all gone and the Hubbard's will be sooner or later too.

As I have said, I was not living at home at the time, but this is what happened.

Eddy had the 1965 June Whitsun Monday off work because it was a Bank Holiday. Dad was working away though, which left my mother and two brothers home together. In the evening Eddy decided to drive to the cinema in Seaford on his motorbike to watch The Return of the Magnificent Seven. He came out of the cinema and was riding along the main road which was a new by-pass back then, from Seaford towards Newhaven.

A van driven by an elderly man accompanied by his wife, drove out of the side road coming from the Buckle seafront direction and turned left towards Newhaven. He said later at the inquest that he did not see anything and thought the road was clear. How on earth can a driver not see a motorbike with its lights on? It was about 10.30pm by then and dark enough for lights. He must have been blind and deaf as well as stupid and definitely too old to be driving. In his seventies actually. However, it was recorded as a RTA (road traffic accident) and no charges were brought against the driver of the van, although my dad did try to make a case and take the driver to court to see justice done.

Apparently he drove right into my brother's passing motorbike, which was on a straight run on a dry road, knocking him clean off and into the roadside ditch, with his helmet still on. This was witnessed by passengers on the bus at the bus stop in front, on the other side of the road to where it happened at Bishopstone. It was reported in the local newspaper, the Evening Argus. Somebody called the police and ambulance although there were no mobile phones back then, and Eddy was taken to the Royal Sussex County Hospital in Brighton but died of internal injuries in the ambulance on the way.

My mother was visited and told by the police, they rang for my father to come home immediately, and my younger brother was in bed asleep. My uncle Rob had to go and identify the body for my parents and he said there was not a mark on him. Mum told me later she was glad Eddy had not ended up as a vegetable, as she put it, and was glad for his sake that he knew nothing about the accident, because the policeman had told her he was knocked unconscious and never recovered.

My mother could not bring herself to go to the funeral service at Brighton crematorium and in due course a Memorial Service was arranged in Rodmell church.

My dad had arranged for us to stay at a local caravan site so we went by train from Paignton to Newhaven where he met us. He lent us his Mini Traveller car to use while we were there, not knowing that my husband only had a provisional driving licence, but we had decided now was not the time to tell him!

We arrived in convoy down The Street in Rodmell, parked the cars and walked up the lane to the church. We went inside and saw it was full. Full of kind caring relations, friends and neighbours who had known us all. That was what Rodmell village was still like in the 1960's. They had left the front two rows of pews free for us family. We sat behind my parents, brother and grandmother. My husband held my hand while I held our toddler who was kept quiet by my great-aunt and uncle sitting behind us. Their commemorative bench seat is in the churchyard just inside the lych gate on the left, next to our row of ancestor's headstones. We had left our three month old baby back at Mum's house in her carrycot by my other gran with her broken leg.

After the church service we all stood outside, to the right of the church doorway where the cremated remains plot is reserved in a small triangular piece of grass. Eddy's ashes were put there in a hole in the ground by the Rector, underneath a rusty nail in the church wall for our future reference. There is a commemorative stone plaque on the wall above with the names of those beneath. This is a place I always visit whenever I am in Sussex. Last year I planted some daffodil bulbs right in the corner of the plot but nobody has told me whether they grew or not.

After that service, I went for that solitary walk to the river to contemplate following in my namesake's footsteps.

As I watched my empty cigarette packet drift slowly downstream I suddenly came to my senses. I pulled myself together and walked quickly away from the lure of the river, back to join my family congregated in Gran's cottage. Unlike my namesake I had two babies to live for so I came back from that black pit of despair, perhaps, to put her words into effect.

"Still, one got over things. Still, life had a way of adding day to day"

A year later in the following June, my eldest son was born, England won the Football World Cup (which we have never managed to do since) and my Rodmell grandmother's ashes were put there too. Some say she never recovered from the shock of Eddy's accident, other people's opinion was that she died of shock after her estranged daughter Audrey flew over from Canada.

Aunt Audrey was the one who married the Canadian soldier after becoming pregnant. When she and her baby boarded a train at Lewes to travel to Liverpool, Gran did not go to wave her off but her dad did. Aunt Audrey sailed on a war bride's ship from Liverpool to Canada. She was met at the other end by her new mother-in-law and lived in Manitoba for the rest of her long life. She had four children, two of each, divorced her husband for alcoholism and got a job in the canteen of a big department store. After about twenty years, her children encouraged her to fly to England to visit her mother. She came alone but her two brothers supervised and chaperoned the visit, which went well so everyone was happy at the time.

"For we think back through our mothers if we are women"

Audrey's dad, who doted on her, had died about ten years previously. It may have been the two shocks, but my personal belief is that Gran was stronger than that and the reason for her demise was more to do with being overweight - her doctor had put her on a diet and she told me to stop posting her Devon Clotted Cream, much as she loved it - together with the fact that she had bad hips and had to walk with a stick, so I think her fall down the stairs had more to do with the state of her health rather than the state of her mind. Which is why she is my role model but I try to watch my weight and walk a lot.

CHAPTER TWELVE

Before the war my mother Florence was living in North London with her parents and sister. She worked as a shop assistant and sometimes modelled the coats, which was usual in those days. She had told me they sold morning clothes and for years I assumed she meant outfits to wear in the mornings but recently I did some research and found out she meant mourning clothes and the coats were made of fur. If you are confused - the answer is in the different spelling of morning and mourning. Nobody objected to animal fur coats back then, mink being the most expensive, indeed there were mink farms, with rabbit fur being the cheap alternative. There were fox fur stoles to drape around women's shoulders, some complete with head and legs. In the 1960s faux fur was invented and from then on wearing animal skins was frowned upon.

Dad had joined the Army before war was declared and was in Wiltshire on training exercises. He had lied about his age to be accepted, stating he was a year older than he actually was. They met in a cinema queue in Trowbridge. Mum was staying with her cousin and Dad was off-duty with a mate. At the end of Mum's holiday she returned to London and they kept in touch. She was the only woman for my dad. He wrote her prolific love letters and they became engaged on one of his Army leaves. Mum was a welcome visitor to his mother's house in Rodmell, where she met his extended family who all welcomed her.

In January 1941, on Dad's birthday, they were married in a London registry office. They had a double ceremony with her sister, who was younger and jealous, so she married her current boyfriend at the same time. Mum continued to live with her parents and sister, while their husbands were away in the war, until soon after I was born. London was still being bombed so we evacuated to Sussex to live with my gran - which I have already told you about.

#######

Married life was good as far as my parents were concerned. They had three children, lived in nice houses, Mum was happy to be a housewife and did not wish to go out to work and Dad built up a good business first as a fencing contractor and then as a builder. As they became more affluent they went out for the evening once a week and took holidays at home and abroad. My gran came to look after us while our parents were away. Mum had all the mod cons she wanted in the house, as well as a weekly cleaning lady after we moved to

Newhaven in 1955, when they bought their first house for £2000, first choosing the plot on Mount Pleasant and then waiting while it was built.

Until in 1966 their lives changed forever when Eddy - my brother and I think their favourite child - was killed. Wrong time, wrong place resulting in a lot of mis-directions and ruined lives.

Not least of which my own children as they hardly ever got to see their grandparents so they had no bond with them. Nor with their paternal grandparents for different reasons. Sometimes they still mention this to me as they have children of their own now and it makes me feel both sad and angry, guilty even. I accept it was fate but it put us all off religion.

Sometime after the death of my brother Dad went to Loch Ness in the Scottish Highlands with a fishing friend hoping to find solace. Instead he found out building land was for sale at reasonable prices, compared to the South East of England, so he moved up there to start a new business leaving my mother and brother behind. After a year of grieving and deliberating, they joined him. Dad had detached himself even more by now because after a time of working with Dad my brother joined the Army and enlisted in the Queens

Own Highlanders where he had to wear a regulation skirt with regulation no underwear on parade. The sergeant walked along the line-up with a mirror on a stick to see if the regulation was kept!

Mum wasn't able to help them, she told me she didn't like being the 'pig in the middle' when they argued. She was always subservient to my dad anyway. I asked her once if she had ever contemplated leaving him and she replied, "Yes, many times." She also told me she fancied a London dentist in her youth and was fancied by a Police Inspector when they lived in Scotland. But she stayed faithful and loyal to my dad to the end. So I copied her attitude.

I miss you so much Mummy, I wish I could hear your voice again and the stories you never told me.

Mum and I were alike inasmuch as we had no wish to live independently. We liked having a man about the house, someone to lean on, someone to be there, someone to talk to and someone to share things with. We were not alike in many other ways though, Mum was quiet and gentle and liked her clothes and hair-do's. She knew how to get her own way by saying, "Yes, dear" and then doing exactly what she wanted whereas I argued believing I was always right. Neither of my parents seemed able or even willing to understand me but I know they loved me and did their best.

Dad asked me once, "We brought you up properly, didn't we?" To which I replied, "Yes, Dad". This was in April 1995 when he knew he was terminally ill with cancer and we were having a talk by a river in Scotland. At that time he told my aunt Josie on the phone, "Virginia will look after Mum when I've gone." She relayed this confidence to me.

My husband and I had driven up to Scotland on one of our twice yearly visits aka holidays and we were greeted with that shattering news of his illness. Mum told Chris in the car in Beauly when Dad and I were in the Spar shop. Then it was his job to tell me when we were alone. Dad died in the Inverness hospice in September, having moved to a smaller bungalow only five weeks before for Mum's sake, and putting his affairs in order i.e. burning most of his marquetry pictures and leaving Mum's birthday present in his workshop. Somebody stole his power drill from there. He was seventy-four.

This is another example of why my book is so named because he was my mum's carer before he became too weak to look after her, then they had to have daily carers so they could continue living in their own home. Mum had rheumatoid arthritis which started when she was about fifty and she became more and more disabled over time. She had to give up knitting but took up crossword puzzles so she did not get dementia like her mother had.

My maternal Gran died in Brighton hospital in 1969 not knowing who her family were, not even her husband. She had become forgetful and incapable so ended her days in the hospital. She had called her husband names and kept leaving the gas on. Grampy lived well into his eighties and went into a care home in Ringmer when he could no longer look after himself in the Lewes flat they had shared. I visited him there, it was a nice place Delves House, situated at the top of the Green where I used to play stoolball.

After my dad died Mum spent many hours on the phone talking to me. Our roles were reversed then, I became her mother figure and she became the needy one, which was perfectly understandable, and I remembered the confidence Dad had about me looking after her. I had turned fifty by then and was finally treated as an adult, I thought to myself.

About a year after losing my dad, Mum lost her left leg. She had to have it amputated because of lack of circulation, even though she never smoked and rarely drank alcohol. Until then, I thought only young men and soldiers had amputations. Of course, we went up there at that time and I spent all the hospital visiting hours with her. I saw a lady in the opposite bed die in front of me. She kept looking at me talking to Mum and didn't drink her tea. After a while I was worried about her so I called a nurse who quickly drew the curtains around her bed and left her there for the rest of visiting time. I wasn't scared as she had quietly and peacefully passed away, unlike my dad who's breathing was heavy and rasping until it suddenly stopped. Then I knew where the saying 'a deathly hush' comes from.

After being discharged Mum carried on living at home in Scotland. We continued visiting and could stay in her house now that Dad was not there. The next year Mum had to have her right leg amputated, this time above the knee, it had got gangrene from an ulcer which wouldn't heal. It was heartbreaking to see it being cleaned by the district nurse and then a plastic bread bag put over the bandages at bath times. She had left it for too long until she felt brave enough to face the operation again knowing what it would mean for her afterwards. But still she continued to live at home with visiting carers in between hospital stays and flatly refused to move down to Devon where we all lived. They would have laid on an ambulance to bring her.

Her heart finally gave out in January 2000; she had been admitted to Inverness hospital with a bad cold and difficulty in breathing - my brother and his partner were staying there for Christmas and New Year - but she never went home again. I was telephoned by the hospital with the unexpected news and my husband drove me to Scotland the next morning. Her last words to me, on her home phone, had been 'Happy - New - Year' in a slow, wheezing, gasping voice but I had not expected her to die. We had arranged for me to go and look after her on her discharge from hospital and she was expecting me.

Before my dad's demise, we were warned on the phone by the hospice and were able to get there in time, although Dad was unconscious. But we had got there in time to be with Mum which is what he would have wanted. He knew we had our train tickets booked but in the event we had to go the night before on the sleeper train, which doubled the cost, and we stayed with Mum for three weeks until she felt strong enough to cope. She had a brilliant friend and a neighbour and her carers.

After Mum died, my brother and his partner, my husband and myself all stayed in Mum's bungalow for three weeks sorting things out. We sent most of the furniture to auction as we only had cars, and we returned all the disability aids. We drove over to the Isle of Skye one Sunday as I knew I would never set foot in Scotland again and I had not been on Skye before. We all left together, my brother carrying both our parents ashes in his car along with their microwave - it was a lame joke that if he got stopped he would have to explain away those three items! He drove home to Sussex and we drove home to Devon.

Several weeks later we met up again in Sussex and with other members of our family scattered our parents ashes together. My father's wish was to have his ashes scattered on top of Mill Hill, where he used to play as a boy, so that is where my parents ashes are, along with my aunt, uncle and sister-in-law. This is why Rodmell was and always will be a special place to me. I do not want to end up there myself because it is too cold and windy up on Mill Hill, besides it is too far for my family to visit when they feel like a little chat or moan. But I wouldn't mind a little bit of me being scattered in Rodmell churchyard one day near Eddy and the rest of me in Torquay Crem; together with their dad, so that we are still around for our family to visit us.

"What does the brain matter compared with the heart?"

My parents were married for fifty-four years and I think they were brave to face their adversities head-on. I hope some of their positive energy has rubbed off on me.

Those latter years were bittersweet for me; on the one hand when there were four of us, (my parents, husband and I), we spent happy holidays staying in different places all over Scotland, sightseeing, walking, touring and eating out but on the other hand I cried like a baby all the way down to Perth after saying goodbye and then sobbed the rest of the way to the English border. It would be another six months before we crossed it again; there was no turning back and it broke my heart every time. During those traumatic years my husband was my anchor, and now I miss him too after spending more than fifty-two years together; he was my other half.

CHAPTER THIRTEEN

It wasn't too difficult to find a one bedroom flat after our bedsits and caravans. Torquay is full of flats, everybody seems to want to live down here, except me. Now I am retired I suppose it suits me better but it will never be my home county like Sussex where my roots are. Maybe I will move back one day, who knows what the future holds? Ideally I would like a modest home with a small garden in both counties. I think I could just about afford two flats, one in each county, but after starting off in private flats I don't want to end up in one. I am not keen on communal living and prefer my own space with my own front door. I could live in a mobile home but you can't rearrange the furniture as it is fitted, and they depreciate in value so that's not a good financial idea. I am keeping an open mind as there are pro's and con's to everything, but if I met someone who was compatible I would not mind sharing my life again, like Rose did; she met somebody else after her husband died, she's enjoying her new life and is older than me. I feel younger now than I did ten years ago. So time will tell, she mused!

# # # # # # #

I found a nice first floor flat in Vicarage Road Chelston, it had big bay windows overlooking the Green, with the kitchen area down that end, and a separate bedroom with a large lounge area in between. Here I knitted baby clothes and had my first baby. This was the best flat and the best landlords we had - but summer loomed and we had to move on again, to another caravan site, this time in Paignton, it was a holiday chalet costing £8 per week which was holiday rates but it was that or nothing.

We went back to Chelston for the next winter where I had baby number two and where I last saw my brother. The wife of the live-in Landlord of this Victorian house that they couldn't really afford, was a mean, nasty woman. She reduced me to tears more than once. We had our rooms along the back of the house with a view of the garden where we tenants were allowed to hang out our washing. The Green was at the front and I recall pushing the pram round it one afternoon crying my eyes out, wishing my husband would get home from work, because Mrs Nasty had taken my baby clothes out of the communal bathroom's airing cupboard and dumped them outside my flat door. I hadn't asked permission to use the cupboard, which would have kept the clothes nice and warm, I only used a corner of it for a pile of baby clothes and she took them out. On my way to the shops

I knocked and asked permission and she said no, it wasn't for tenants use. I had two small girls in the pram which had been a real struggle to get down the stairs and was upset. I went into the park instead of heading to the shops and cried with frustration, anger, tiredness and misery. Then off to another caravan site for the summer in due course, and so it went on. However, salvation was on the horizon.

After over two years on the waiting list and a lot of letters from me, the local council offered us a Prefab in Hele. A home of our own at last, instead of never-ending moving from pillar to post. And plenty of space, with a proper kitchen, a nice lounge with a French door, two bedrooms, a proper bathroom all to ourselves and a wrap around garden with two gates and a shed. I was happy there, which lasted for about eighteen months. I taught myself how to hang wallpaper and paint woodwork, we tended the garden and grew potatoes, onions, runner beans and tomatoes. Strawberries were growing there already. We even got a dog and I could hang the washing out on my own line, he used to chase it when it was flapping dry. I had baby number three there, a boy. I am writing this bit on his birthday; the 15th of June.

One day we received a letter from the council informing us that the prefabs were being demolished to make way for new houses but they would re-house us - somewhere. Okay, an unavoidable move was now on the cards. Sadly so because we had made friends with the neighbours, got to know everybody else (who were also given notice) and got used to the local shops. There was a swing park in a big field just up the road and it was a reasonable distance to walk into town. My sister-in-law Rose lived nearby too.

We were allowed up to three choices of location for our three bedroom brick built council house, but I accepted the first one offered after I went and viewed it. Chris didn't like Watcombe as he was a Hele village boy, but I must have liked it because it was our family home for thirty years. We had two more children there, both boys. After twenty years when the youngest left school, we exercised our Right To Buy made possible by the then Prime Minister Margaret Thatcher.

It was an end terrace house on an estate outside of Torquay just off the coast road to Teignmouth, close to Watcombe beach, Brunel woods and the countryside, an ideal place to bring up children. I kept up the routine my mother had taught me, she had never gone out to work, except for two weeks when she covered for me at the doctors' surgery in Seaford while I had my annual holiday. She didn't like going out to work and wouldn't do it again she said, mainly because when she got home my father and two brothers were sitting there waiting to be fed!

My life was a continuous slog of the same routine week after week, revolving around school times, housework, shopping and cooking. I hardly ever had time to sit down until the children were asleep, but even then, being a night owl, I would go in the garden on summer evenings and potter about. In the winter I would knit - jumpers, cardigans, hats, gloves and scarves. Reading or listening to the radio or music was a thing of the past, but we would watch television together in the evenings after dinner. My habit was to leave the washing-up until the mornings, so Chris always did it after bringing me a cup of tea in bed. That's another thing I miss. When the eldest were at secondary school and the youngest started primary school, I got part-time hotel work to supplement our income, and when the youngest went to secondary school I had European students in the summer months as well. Our very first student was Ludovica from Rome and we had a Firenza car at the time, which pleased her enormously, after that we usually had German girls.

The children still had a free-range childhood back in the 1970s, unlike today's children. It was not much different from my own, except we had a car so went out as a family for Sunday afternoon drives after our roast dinner, usually over Dartmoor. We didn't like them playing out on Sundays, even though I had felt really disappointed when my parents made me go to Sunday School instead of to Tide Mills beach with my friends when I was growing up in Newhaven. Being a parent now though, I understood the need for structure and discipline, love and attention, as well as good food, clean clothes and a clean home. So that is why I was kept busy.

The house was spacious and the rooms were square, the three boys shared a bedroom at the front of the house, we had the back bedroom because I liked the view over to the woods, my eldest daughter had the ground floor bedroom and my other daughter had the single bedroom. We had a separate toilet and bathroom upstairs with another toilet downstairs. The lounge, with an open fire, was at the back of the house leading into the garden via a French door and we converted the old adjoining coal shed into a utility room. All the boots and shoes had to be stored there or in the meter cupboard under the stairs.

For the last ten years there we were buying it so could lavish it with lots of DIY and home improvements. This gave me free rein to experiment with the aid of books and magazines because television did not cover house programmes like it does today. I watch them avidly now, always on the lookout for new ideas and often rearrange the furniture, only to come downstairs in the mornings and put it all back again!

Finally, all the children left home; they either got married, had partners or set up on their own, just like I did once, although my independence only lasted a few days. We decided to downsize to a two bedroom bungalow in Paignton where they were cheaper than in Torquay. All rooms on one floor with no stairs - except I didn't like sleeping downstairs and it seemed odd not having an upstairs so we converted the loft, making it into an en suite master bedroom. This was successful as it freed up space for a dining room downstairs, but the downside was sleeping in the roof space gives you surround sound with the seagulls tap dancing and squawking on the roof and passing traffic, it was noisy to say the least. Mary the neighbour was like a sentry on duty at the top of our steps whenever we went in or out or up and down, waylaying us for a chat, so we nicknamed her 'Nosey Mary'. Her husband had warned us about her and he was not wrong.

The garden was very steep and well-stocked both at the back and front and Chris built a fishpond. I liked the far reaching views from the top and the steps gave me plenty of exercise. We lived opposite a row of local shops which was fine at the beginning until an off-licence opened up in what was a hairdressing salon opposite my lounge picture window. I did not like the way it was open until late at night and seven days a week so after eight years there, I decided we had to move.

I found an affordable house for sale in Stoke, my daughter's village. By this time she had a family and I thought it would be nice if we lived close by so we moved out into the sticks. This house had three bedrooms again but it was a mid-terrace, so I felt like I had no elbow room and they were not well soundproofed. Not being the neighbourly type I didn't like being overlooked and here I felt surrounded. Being near to my daughter and granddaughters was lovely though and I enjoyed babysitting, collecting them from the village nursery school, supervising the swimming pool, running around the garden and playing games with them. But the neighbour from hell moved in next door to us to complement the noisy, scruffy family on the other side so after only two years I felt I had to get out of there before I got depressed again or went mad, instead of complaining to hubby all the time. He didn't seem to mind it there but he had wheels.

Here, in the beautiful seaside resort of Babbacombe, I have lived in this old fisherman's cottage for eight years. It was built around 1860, is in a good location, a few hundred yards from the beach, which is very steep to walk down to, or there is the Cliff Railway to take people up and down. The cottage is on flat ground with no fear of flooding, in a row of similar properties. All the amenities are a short walk away and the neighbours are quiet. There is only one thing wrong with it in my opinion; it's in the wrong county!

"For women live much more in the past,
they attach themselves to places"

THE END

ACKNOWLEDGEMENTS

I wrote this autobiographical memory book over a period of four months, as therapy for myself and a legacy for my children, soon after becoming a widow after fifty-one years of marriage to the same man; a feat in itself. I decided it would be easier to think about the distant past than the recent past. I have changed most of the names to protect the innocent.

With grateful thanks to:

Lana Hall, my inspiration
Virginia Woolf, author
Nils Visser, editor, publisher and author
Frank Patterson, cover artist
Corin Spinks, cover editor
Lesley Bourke, editor and proof-reader
Lesley Carrington, technician and proof-reader

Without their help and encouragement along the way this book would not have been written.

Last but not least, I thank you, the reader.

ANCESTRY APPENDIX

As I mentioned in the acknowledgements one of the reasons for writing this book is to leave a legacy for my family and the following information is relevant to that purpose.

The history of Rodmell windmill. This wooden post mill is long gone but it was built up on Mill Hill around 1800. Rodmell village is in two parts, divided by the main road and sloping down from the South Downs to the river Ouse. The mill stood at the highest point from where you can see over to Telscombe village with Brighton town beyond.

The first mill owner was John Fuller. In 1810 he sold it to John Glazebrook whose son William worked the mill for fifty years. In 1877 his executors sold the mill to Jacob Verrall. In 1911 he sold it on to George Skinner who had already been Verrall's tenant since 1902. By 1912 the mill was under-used and in poor condition so Skinner and his two sons demolished it and sold the wood to a local building firm.

In 1871 an ancestor of mine, James Deadman, was playing outside the mill while his father was working inside, he was hit on the head and knocked over by one of the sweeps. He went to hospital with a head injury and broken arm but made a full recovery. There had been a windmill at Rodmell since medieval times so 1912 was the end of an era.

I would like to get one thing straight, the origin of my ancestral surname has nothing to do with dead men. It reputedly comes from Debenham in Norwich and derives from living 'near the river' hence *Deadman*. Thankfully around 1900 someone had the foresight to drop the *a* so now I come from the *Dedmans*. What with *Hubbard* being my other ancestral surname I do not come from a very illustrious heritage, but I am proud that I have Sussex roots and was lucky enough to grow up in that beautiful county.

########

Rodmell village has variously been known as Redmelle or Ramelle in the 11th century, Redmelde in the 12th century, Radmelde in the 13th century, Radmill in the 18th century, Rodmill in the 19th century and from then on Rodmell, as it is today. The name probably derives from 'mylde' meaning (the place of) red mud. This makes sense because there was a Pottery at Mill House at the bottom of Mill Lane near the main road. From about 1954 to 1962 it was run by Judith Partridge and her pottery can still be found for sale; it is now a collectable. The pottery was made a listed building in 1965 and is now a private house called, unsurprisingly: The Old Pottery.

I have traced my Sussex ancestors back to 1720 without much trouble, thanks to the internet, and found my earliest recorded ancestor was Thomas who married Elizabeth in 1745 in Ovingdean near Brighton. Their fourth son Richard was born about 1758 in Sussex, baptised in Falmer and married Sarah in Rodmell. He was a shepherd and his family originated from Brighton, roaming the South Downs looking for work tending sheep. I presume Sarah was a Rodmell girl and they were married in her local church in her home village which was called Rodmill in those days.

There was a church in Rodmell at the time of the Doomsday Book. St. Peter's church is early Norman although the font is thought to be Saxon, which is earlier. I was christened in Southease church (which has an unusual round tower), just along the road because one Rector covered both villages. The Rectory is an imposing Queen Anne residence with a large rear garden, about halfway down The Street, I have been in there to play with the Rector's two daughters. The current Rector lives in Kingston another village past Northease in the opposite direction to Southease. The Old Rectory is now a private residence.

I am descended through James who was born and baptised in Rodmill in 1791, he married Sarah in 1817, they had seven children and he died in 1873. Their son Thomas was born in 1827, he married another Sarah and died in 1908. This was about the same time they changed their surname so my great-grandfather is William Thomas Dedman who was born in 1865 and died in 1953 at the ripe old age of eighty eight. He must have seen a lot of changes in his lifetime although he never left the village. You might remember him from where I have previously written about the Woolfs, because it was he who was their gardener when they first went to live in Rodmell.

In 1881 William was in the census as living at 14 Street Rodmell, and he was listed as a Roadman in the 1901 census. He married Rachel Ann West, who took meals to the Woolfs if you remember. They had nine children, William, Alex, Henry, Jessie, Elsie, Dorothy, Florence, Albert and James. Florence, my grandmother, was born in January 1892. The Dedman lineage finally died out in Rodmell in 1984 when my great-uncle James, the youngest of the siblings, died. They lived in the first house in The Dicklands off Mill Lane. He was a chauffeur and gardener. He left a wife Ellen, who died in about 2000 and their two children moved away from the village. Another aunt and uncle also lived in The Dicklands in one of the middle houses but they emigrated to Australia in 1951, she was Aunt Eileen, my long-distance godmother. Her mother was my gran's sister Dorothy who lived in 1 Vine Cottages halfway down The Street. They also bought No. 2 at a later date for their son and his family. We lived in The Cottage up a side lane. My estranged grandfather lived round The Loop opposite Pear Tree cottage and my great-grandparents lived down the bottom by the Brooks in Briar cottage. My family were spread all over Rodmell in the days of yore.

I really appreciate feedback. Please visit me on:

Facebook:

https://www.facebook.com/Rachel-West-1623740914564329/timeline/

Pinterest:

https://www.pinterest.com/2185hall/onwards-and-downwards/

Lightning Source UK Ltd.
Milton Keynes UK
UKHW041831131019
351534UK00001B/10/P